THE BBC RADIO SUSSEX GUIDE TO

Hidden Sussex

by
WARDEN SWINFEN
and
DAVID ARSCOTT

with line drawings by
JOHN WHITING

THIS STONE WAS ERECTED
TO THE MEMORY
FRED HUGHES
WHO WORKED THESE FIELDS AND LOVED THEM,
HE BUILT THE FARM YOU SEE
AND NEVER WANTED ANY MORE
ONLY TO BE FREE
1906~1978

BBC RADIO SUSSEX
1 MARLBOROUGH PLACE, BRIGHTON
1984

This book is dedicated to all the people who have helped us in our quest, and especially to the Standens of Horsted Keynes, and to Tony, without whom it would never have even begun.

ISBN 0 9509510 0 5

Photoset and printed in England by Flexiprint Ltd., Worthing, Sussex.

Cover photograph by Anthony J. Standen.

YOUR TRUE adventurer may be happier to travel than to arrive, but few of us are sufficiently gipsy of spirit to set out with no idea of our destination. We like to aim for something. We like to be guided. A sorry consequence is that a few celebrated haunts are overrun with visitors, to the neglect of the hundreds of villages and hamlets which have their own, unsung, beauties and curiosities. The herd mentality has evidently bedevilled motoring from the outset:

> *At the wheel of your car, the engine*
> *running smoothly, you spin along*
> *through village after village, admiring*
> *the view, and often missing a vista*
> *which a turn down a bye-lane would*
> *give you — losing an old church or*
> *castle which a halt by a gate and a few*
> *yards' walk would show your party . . . .*

This observation appeared in one of the first motorists' guides ever to be published in Sussex — by the garage firm, Caffyns, who (more than 50 years later) are the generous sponsors of our own book. Various routes were suggested to entice drivers from the main thoroughfares, so that hikers tramping those bye-lanes must have been disagreeably surprised to meet the fuming roadsters of the time, but I think it fair to claim that we have been rather more ambitious. After all, we set out to investigate every single village in what is a very large county, and we have found something to say about nearly 400 of them.

All book titles are traps for their creators. There is clearly nothing 'hidden' about the Balcombe Viaduct, or Jack and Jill up on their windy hill. Mad Jack Fuller undoubtedly meant his follies to be noticed — in one case money depended upon it. But our title meets the majority of cases. We have, for the most part, concentrated on the miniature rather than the grand, the particular rather than the general. We have avoided the towns and those villages which have an urban character: these have been fulsomely praised, where they deserve it, and can look after themselves. We all know, more or less, what to expect from Chichester, Lewes and Brighton. We shall find ample guides to places such as Arundel and Rye. Who, on the other hand, has thought to celebrate a humble wooden cross in an overgrown churchyard; the house-leeks sprouting on an hospitable roof; a rusting loco at an abandoned station; or the chandelier purchased with coins from the purse of a drowned child?

Some of the objects we point out are strange or striking in themselves; others have a tale to tell. But we trust that when you go village-hunting with this book in your hands (leaving the second copy by your bedside) you will resist the temptation simply to tick off the items and jump back into the car. This is new territory: explore it! Our researches have involved us in plenty of reading and in talking to many observant friends of Radio Sussex (too many to mention) but the greatest pleasure of all has been in driving around the county, alert of eye and ear.

Having produced and presented local radio programmes for several years, I had imagined myself to be fairly well-acquainted with the county: a smugness that was soon to be severely chastened. Warden Swinfen — in every respect the senior partner in our enterprise — had a similar experience. An assiduous explorer of Sussex, well known to regular listeners for his contributions about the museum world, he too was to learn something at every turn. How far we are still lacking we shall soon discover. We confidently expect sacks of mail, berating us for the obvious things we have overlooked. Cost prevents us from including blank pages in our guide, but we would ask you to regard it very much as an incomplete scrapbook. Add to it yourself as you go along — in the margins of your third copy.

We assume that you have a map. Our own sketch (page 14) and numbering system should help you to locate each entry without too much difficulty, though precise instructions would have become tedious and wasteful of space. Chinwagging a native over the fence will on occasion be necessary — and will doubtless bring its own rewards. Although all the places we mention may be approached without breaking the law of the land, few of them are suitable for coach-loads of rampant sightseers. We pray that no owner of a fascinating private property who confronts a stranger with his nose to the window, no farmer whose livestock is pestered by unleashed dogs, no churchwarden following a trail of muddy footprints to the chancel, will find the culprit carrying a copy of this book. Please tread respectfully wherever you go.

A final word about our sources. We have driven thousands of miles seeking original material. We have visited the villages, spoken to people with good local knowledge and read our books (a few of which are noted in a condensed bibliography). We have striven for accuracy. Where we have repeated colourful legends and engaging tall stories we have indicated our reservations, perhaps less from a regard for Truth itself than from a fear of sharing with that early Caffyns author the knowing smiles of a later generation. The skull found at Piltdown he described as that of 'a man of the Pleistocene age . . . the oldest in existence', though it was originally, he informs us with a tolerant lack of censure, 'believed to be the skull of an ape'. Unlucky scribe! I here place on record our doubts about the dreaded Knucker in its watery hole, the voracious appetite of the giant Bevis.

David Arscott

INTRODUCTION

THE RICHNESS of experience which our lovely county can offer was only one of the lessons which compiling this book has taught us. A cottage in this village, a church in that, a view near another, have all been entered in our notebooks. Then, by careful sifting at leisure, we have tried to reflect the variety we have found. We have not aimed at complete cataloguing — by recording an oasthouse at Boreham Street or a dovecote at Patcham, and writing a sentence or two about them, we are not implying that others — perhaps better ones — cannot be found elsewhere.

The richness of Sussex is an ordered richness. Our captures have tended to fall into certain categories — which may be the result of our own approach. In travelling around we found that the best help came from vicars, postmistresses (more numerous than postmasters, for some reason) and innkeepers. We could easily have written a County Guide to Good Ploughman's Lunches, but the pattern has developed differently. Our basic plan has been to make for the church as a starting point. Often we have found in it enough to use all our available space: this book could have been filled with notes about features in Sussex churches, but that has been ably done by other and more learned writers. Mindful, however, that others may not share our enthusiasms, we have passed over many more churches than we have mentioned, in favour of some more eye-catching curiosity. It seemed essential to include an index of subjects so that a thread of interest could be pursued through an entanglement of place names in alphabetical order.

Most forcibly we have learnt that the richness of Sussex is inexhaustible. As my friend David Arscott says in his preface, we set out to investigate every single village. On our visiting days we encountered many whose names do not appear in these pages, but we cannot claim to have seen everything. There has always been another unexplored road to drive down, always another unfamiliar name on a signpost. Given another six months, I am confident that we could have added another hundred names to our lists. Perhaps their turn will come in the fullness of time.

If, as we believe, it will be useful to offer a few introductory generalisations about the kinds of 'notabilia' we have collected, we must begin with the natural features. The geography of Sussex runs in horizontal strips from east to west. In the north is a high ridge of gently rolling upland which includes the area around Blackdown, the forests of St. Leonard's, Worth, Ashdown and others, and the 'beacons' at Colgate, Wych Cross and Crowborough. Above this ridge is a strip of flatter country only a few miles wide before it laps over into Surrey. South of it is the Weald, a plain of rich heavy soil which once used to be so thickly wooded that the Roman armies preferred to go round it rather than through it. In the eastern half of the county it reaches the coast between Eastbourne and Hastings. South again is the chalk ridge of the South Downs, running not quite parallel to the coast: it is a few miles inland at the Hampshire border, while eastward it soars out into the sea in the cliffs of the Seven Sisters (see *Birling*) and Beachy Head, just west of Eastbourne. The northern face of the Downs is steeper than the southern, as can be dramatically seen by motorists on the A27 road east of Lewes. It is towards the north that one must look for the finest views from 'beacons' such as Firle and Ditchling, from Highdown and the Rings at Chanctonbury and Cissbury. The difference in soil is obvious even to the comparatively casual observer, with the clay of the Weald affording luxuriant banks of rhododendrons and azaleas and other plants which cannot tolerate the alkali of chalk and lime. Then in the far south-west, around Chichester and Bosham, and in the south-east are flat alluvial areas with many a sheltering harbour or river creek.

The coastal strip has undergone many transformations. In prehistoric times there was no sea between England and France: the English Channel was formed in Mesolithic (Middle Stone Age) times, quite recently by geological standards. But far more recently, substantial changes have continued to occur. The River Ouse met the sea at Seaford until late Tudor times, but after a great storm in 1579 it broke through the shingle bank and altered course dramatically. It left Seaford so completely that a new harbour had to be built — hence the name New Haven, or Newhaven. There had indeed been some development of New Haven as a port a few years earlier; it had hitherto been known as Meeching, and the name New Haven is first recorded in 1566.

Shoreham harbour too was made useless when the Adur moved its mouth further east. We mention under *Middleton* and *Winchelsea* some other instances of coastal change in the two halves of the county. The process is of course still continuing; were it not so, there would be no need for the massive timber or concrete groynes we see along our beaches.

The first people of Sussex avoided the impenetrable forests of the lower ground and lived mainly on the uplands. From Stone Age and Iron Age times there are dozens of major sites along the Downs — hundreds if one counts isolated tumuli, or burial mounds — while those so far discovered in the lower woodland areas can be counted on the fingers of one hand. No doubt this was partly due to the availability of flint on the hills. Flint is a remarkable material capable of being chipped to a fine cutting edge in skilled hands, yet extremely durable in use. But it weathers readily when exposed, and flints gathered on the surface are of poorer quality than those even a few feet underneath. So our neolithic forbears developed quite sophisticated mining techniques, often sinking shafts to a depth of fifty feet or more and working the stone from radiating horizontal galleries, dumping the rubble from each excavation into its predecessor. Some districts were found to be rich in flints from which could be made knives, cleavers, scrapers, chisels, arrowheads and other tools, and many shafts would be sunk. On some of the hills in the region behind Worthing — Highdown, Blackpatch Hill, Findon Hill, Cissbury and so on — hundreds of pits, often almost overlapping, testify to the importance of the industry, which may have occupied the full time of nearly a quarter of the adult male population. People would have lived in small communities, but of these all too little is known, for the material they used for building their primitive homes has entirely perished. The development of metal working in Bronze Age and Iron Age times is unlikely to have brought about any radical change in their ways of living. Farming was, however, becoming a more significant part of the economy since its introduction to Britain somewhere between 4000 and 3500 BC, coupled with the domestication of cattle, sheep and poultry.

Conditions changed after the coming of the Romans. Once the initial period of military activity was over, Britain became one of the more placid Roman provinces. Officials sent from Rome cleared spaces and built themselves comfortable homes with central heating, baths and mosaic floors. A good number of the native population found Roman ways to their liking and adopted a Roman life-style, even if on a humbler scale. Many traces of the Roman occupation from the first to fourth centuries AD have been found, and no doubt there are more awaiting discovery. They range from the vast palace of a Romanized British prince named Cogidubnus at *Fishbourne,* west of Chichester, through the castle at *Pevensey* and the villa at *Bignor,* to smaller remains which have been excavated at Sompting, Angmering and elsewhere.

In such a civilised community, good roads were necessary for purposes of trade, policing, and, in case of need, military action. Stane Street ran in the west of the county from London to Chichester (see *Adversane*), and other major roads went down to Lewes and Brighton. A number of interconnecting east-west roads created a very serviceable network. Parts of these roads or at least the line of them, survive in too many places for us to provide full logging, but we mention several of them in these pages.

When the Romans departed in the early fifth century they left behind a cultural climate which substantially persisted for several centuries despite the seldom-distant threat of invasion, and was destroyed only by the very different culture of the Vikings from Scandinavia and the Saxons from North Germany. The Saxons had adopted Christianity and their craftsmen spread widely over England, occupying themselves largely in building homes and churches. Of their private buildings scarcely any trace has survived, but the churches, being of stone, are in many cases still very much with us. Perhaps more would have lasted if the hand of Man, the great destroyer, had been less heavy. Even so, there are Saxon churches of the first order of importance at *Worth, Sompting* and *Bosham,* and remains of many more. By tradition, Bosham was the scene of Canute's command to the sea to retreat, and the fact of the king's being in Sussex at all gives a good indication of the importance of the county in Saxon times.

The Norman Conquest was politically a watershed in English history, but culturally its effects were slower in infiltrating. Craftsmen and artists from northern France had been working and even settling in Britain for at least a quarter of a century before 1066. So slow was the general speed of communication then that workers in the remoter parts of England still clung to 'traditional' Anglo-Saxon styles until well after 1100. This timelag is commonly called the 'Saxo-Norman overlap', a phrase which will be met several times in these pages. In terms of architecture in Sussex, the semi-circular arch was the dominant feature until as late as 1200 AD. After that date a point begins to appear at the apex of the arch, modestly at first but gradually increasing in sharpness over the next three hundred years or so.

Survivals are mostly of religious buildings, whose stone construction has proved durable enough to give us some idea of their original appearance. Not entirely, though, because we are so used to seeing bare walls that we accept them as historically accurate, whereas in medieval times they would have been extensively painted with biblical scenes and stories of the saints. The churches at *Hardham* and *Clayton* have extensive twelfth-century paintings which are of national significance, and examples in varying condition can be seen at *Aldingbourne, Coombes* and *West Chiltington,* among other places.

Religious life assumed many forms in medieval times. Sussex has but few traces of pre-Conquest monasticism, but very soon after 1066 the Cluniac order was introduced by William de Warenne, a follower of the Conqueror, who founded Lewes priory in 1077 (see *Southover*). At *Boxgrove*, a Benedictine foundation, enough of the monastic buildings remain to make a visit rewarding, and there are smaller survivals elsewhere, including a nunnery at *Easebourne*. But the most impressive ruins lie on the eastern brink of the county, at *Bayham*, comparing favourably with at least the smaller of the great Cistercian foundations of Yorkshire. To some people the communal life of a monastery lacked appeal, and these might opt for the total seclusion of an anchorite's cell. There are visible remains at *Kingston Buci*, and several churches have records of a hermit, male or female, even though no trace of the actual cell exists.

Sussex is an awkward shape, its east-west dimension being at least four times greater than north-south. Even today the drive from Westbourne to Rye takes all of three hours. Administratively, the county has been divided in two separate areas, east and west, since 1865, but smaller divisions are much older. The earliest political unit in Sussex was the 'hundred', an area in which roughly a hundred families were comprised. This unit is of early Saxon origin, and, although many boundaries have been altered, the concept of a local entity has been maintained through the medieval 'manor' to the 'parish', which still exists for ecclesiastical purposes. The hundreds, of which sixty were named in Domesday, were in turn grouped together as 'rapes', a peculiarly Sussex word apparently of Icelandic origin. These divisions were certainly known to the Normans and may date from before the Conquest — a matter around which much controversy has raged. From earliest days the rapes have been six in number — three in West Sussex (Chichester, Arundel, Bramber) and three in East (Lewes, Pevensey, Hastings). In each Rape there was a river, a harbour, a castle near the coast for defence and an important church, and all stretched from the extreme north of the county to the coast, covering roughly equal areas.

Since a large, though not we hope an overwhelming, number of our entries are connected with churches, we have tried to vary the texture, as it were, by selecting different features for comment in each one. All the same, certain points of interest recur in many churches because they were an integral part of the pattern of worship. In the Middle Ages time was not so important as we find it today, and approximations were 'near enough'. Most churches had a sundial by which the priest could judge when a service such as Mass should begin. These 'mass dials' are fairly common, although nearly always the central pin, or gnomon, is missing. Dials are usually found near a south porch or vestry door, although often stones have been moved during rebuilding, and we noted at least two instances of these 'scratch dials' being situated where no sun ever reaches.

Inside a church, the most obvious feature is the dividing line between the nave, where the congregation sits, and the chancel, where the clergy and choir are positioned to conduct the service. In the chancel may be found a piscina, which was a small recess with a drainhole used for washing the sacred vessels used at Mass; sedilia, seats — from one to three in number — for officiating clergy; and of course the altar itself. Often the chancel is entered through an archway across which a screen was placed before the Reformation in the sixteenth century. High over the screen might have been a rood, a figure of Christ on the Cross, with Mary and John the Baptist on either side. On some solemn days part of the service might be carried out on or beside the screen, and on one side of the chancel arch a little staircase, the rood-stair, was provided. If the chancel arch is so placed that it cuts off the view of the altar from part of the nave, a 'squint' may be inserted; this is a small opening which affords a sight of the priest during the celebration of Mass. Sometimes a squint becomes like a tunnel; that at *West Chiltington* is exceptionally long.

Although even a skeleton history of medieval architecture is beyond the scope of this book, one feature, the 'weeping chancel', must be mentioned, if only to put the record straight. One often sees that the chancel is at a slight angle to the nave — *Bosham* is an extreme instance. It may be off-line either way, and the romantic explanation is sometimes advanced that the deviation corresponds to the angle of Christ's head as He hung on the Cross. This pleasant idea will not, however, bear scrutiny, and much has been written about it. The real explanation is simply that medieval masons were not, and had no need to be, over-scrupulous about setting out lines of foundations. If there was a slight kink, it didn't matter.

By the time of the Tudors in the later fifteenth century there were, by and large, enough churches for the then population. Many seem needlessly large to our eyes, but until the seventeenth century church attendance was virtually compulsory every week, so that big congregations were the rule; and it must also be remembered that shifts in the population have occurred since then. Now that the land was rich and powerful enough to enjoy a period of peace and stability, attention turned to the construction of more substantial homes and other secular buildings. Mature wood was ruthlessly cut from the forests to make the timber-framed houses which fortunately survive in comparative abundance: which is why large stretches of Ashdown and other 'forests' are now open scrub and heath, denuded of the majestic trees they once had. Our cataloguing of timber-framed houses has had to be selective, as there are quite literally hundreds still standing alongside our roads. Many are not in villages or hamlets at all, but they lie on their own, set a little back from the roadside between two places, seemingly belonging to neither of them. They range from modest cottages such as farmhands would have occupied to substantial yeomen's houses built partly of brick, either of level courses or with the herringbone infilling known as 'nogging'. These were clearly intended to be a family home for generations, where a landowner could always oversee the use of his property.

Sussex in the sixteenth century was not, however, an exclusively agricultural county. Deposits of iron ore had been discovered in several areas of the Weald and a sizeable industry developed, lasting in some places until the early years of the nineteenth century. The techniques involved in manufacturing iron products necessitated the construction of furnaces and forges for almost every community. Names like Furnace Wood and Forge Cottage are to be found liberally sprinkled over the Ordnance maps. For the work, a good supply of water also was needed, not only for tempering the metal but for producing the energy required to work the heavy hammers — whence came the 'hammerponds' often mentioned in these pages. Many of the most picturesque old houses in our county were built for substantial iron-masters, as is shown by the presence of a largish pond nearby. Where water-power was inadequate or unreliable, a donkey-wheel might afford a valuable supplement (see *Saddlescombe*). The Sussex iron industry was a major feature of the economic life of the country, manufacturing everything from horseshoes through milestones, firebacks, grave slabs, domestic and agricultural implements up to large cannon and tools of war. Again, the Sussex clay was found to be excellent for the making of bricks, and in several places we note the survival of kilns, often in isolated locations, for brickmaking, the burning of lime, or the production of other building materials.

Eventually the Industrial Revolution sounded the death-knell of Sussex iron; the last forge, at *Ashburnham,* closed about 1820. In brickmaking, too, mass-production has had its part in forcing the abandonment of nearly all the local kilns. There remain only a handful of large concerns — bricks at *Warnham* and *Southwater,* cement at Shoreham, gypsum at *Mountfield,* to mention some at random — to carry the whole load. For a comparatively short time another industry was established — the making of gunpowder — but Sussex continued to rely as heavily as ever upon its staple occupation, agriculture. Many improvements have been initiated by men of Sussex: John Ellman with his Southdown sheep (see *Glynde*) and a Mr. Woods, whose Christian name seems to be unrecorded, with his improved wheat (see *Chidham*), are just two instances. The heavy, fertile soils yielded abundant crops of cereal which needed the labours of millers to make flour, and mills in which to do it. Many remains of this most typical village industry still exist — records of windmills and watermills of varying kinds can be found in the majority of small communities. We mention with pleasure that the preponderance of surviving mills now have bands of enthusiasts restoring them, caring for them and getting them working for the enjoyment of visitors during the summer months.

Brewing increased in importance during the eighteenth century, and hops became a staple crop in Kent and East Sussex. The plant twines its way up an elaborate structure of poles and string, still often seen in the fields around Bodiam. Hop-picking used to be a regular holiday for Londoners (see *Boreham Street*), and after the flowers were picked they were dried in a special oven. This was cylindrical in shape, with a tapering upper cone and a vent on top which was turned by a wind-vane with the prevailing wind. At the top of the cylinder a net of horse hair called an oast-hair was stretched; the hop flowers were spread across it in a thin layer so that they would dry evenly in the warmth of the fire below. Now that sophisticated drying machines have taken over, many oast houses have been converted into living rooms, although care has been taken to preserve their exterior appearance.

In the mid-eighteenth century, however, another new industry was introduced — health. Already the virtues of mineral springs were well known and places like Tunbridge Wells and Bath were popular resorts; but about 1750 a Dr. Russell (see *South Malling*), who had a practice in Lewes, began to extol the benefits of sea bathing. Although he died in 1759, he had been successful in setting up a clinic in Brighton. The idea caught on. Almost overnight, it seems, Royalty 'discovered' the seaside for health and enjoyment and the Sussex tourist industry was born. Other towns sprang up, Hastings, Eastbourne and Worthing among the most prosperous. The process began of turning our coastal strip into a residential area in winter and a holiday centre in summer. The phenomenon of *Peacehaven* after the 1914 war ought to have demonstrated the disasters of such a policy, but still in 1984 the hoardings of estate developers besmirch our countryside not only along the coast but at inland towns such as Horsham, Crawley and Crowborough. Perhaps this book will be the last chance to record the individuality of the more intimate Sussex.

The pattern of agriculture has changed substantially during the same period; the sheep population of the Downs, for example, has varied greatly even within living memory. Numbers fell between the two world wars but nowadays the fields in the more rural areas support substantial numbers not only of sheep but also of cattle. In lower parts an abundance of springs (see *Fulking*) and small streams ensured adequate water for them, but on the Downs a problem arose, to be solved by the making of dewponds. These are man-made pools about which much has been written and much scientific controversy raged. The principle is that a hollow is scooped out of the ground and lined with straw and clay. It is claimed that this excludes the warmth of the surrounding soil, thus making the air in the hollow colder and causing condensation which slowly fills the pool. Once it is filled, the cool fresh water is held even in dry summers, and it is not fed by any springs. Kipling tells us of 'the dewpond on the height, unfed, that never fails'; they make ideal watering-places for roaming livestock.

Through the ages Sussex has been proud to be the home of innumerable great people. Cogidubnus has been mentioned and so has Canute. From the Saxon period come nearly all the Sussex saints, of whom Wilfrid was the most important (see *Selsey*). He lived from 634 to 709, and was a man of strong principles, enduring energy and a cutting tongue — none of them traits calculated to endear him to authority. He was also, Bede tells us, a charming person, handsome, pious and learned. He was Bishop of Ripon until he had violent differences with King Ecgfrith of Northumbria for which he was imprisoned and afterwards banished. He sailed round the coast and landed at Selsey; at Church Norton is a thirteenth century chapel claimed as the successor to the one in which Wilfrid worshipped. He remained in Sussex until Ecgfrith's death five years later and then returned to Northumbria: but in the period of his stay he implanted the Christian religion firmly among the 'undriveable' folk of Sussex.

Then there was St. Cuthman, the 'boy with the cart' of Christopher Fry's verse play. He was an eighth-century shepherd boy from the West country, who came to *Steyning* in search of food, trundling his mother in a home-made wheelbarrow. Here the cord of his cart broke, a sign which he took to mean that he should found a church on the very spot. In those days the Adur was navigable well inland and Steyning used to be known as St. Cuthman's Port until the estuary silted up so that ships could no longer penetrate thus far. Other saintly folk whose names have come down to us include Dicul (see *Boxgrove*), St. Lewinna (see *Alfriston*), and St. Dunstan (see *Mayfield*).

After the Battle of Hastings the Conqueror parcelled out vast tracts of England among his followers. Two families in particular have associations with Sussex — de Warenne and de Braose. Of their domestic circumstances nothing survives, but we can still see the splendid achievements of their castle-builders at *Bodiam* and *Herstmonceux*, and their church masons at Bramber and Shoreham. Apart from the noble families of the Middle Ages whose titles reflected their Sussex origins — Earls of Sussex, Arundel, Chichester and so on — few names have come down to us from before Elizabethan times. But since then distinguished residents of the county have included the lawyer John Selden (*High Salvington*), the dramatist Thomas Otway (*Trotton*), the poets Shelley (*Broadbridge Heath*) and Blake (*Felpham*), the composers Edward Elgar (*Fittleworth*), John Ireland (*Amberley*) and Arnold Bax (*Storrington*, where also lived the poet Francis Thompson), the artists Turner (*Petworth*), Frank Brangwyn (Brighton) and Arthur Rackham (*Houghton*), the sculptor Eric Gill (*Ditchling*), and Richard Cobden, campaigner against the Victorian Corn Laws (*Heyshott*). Tennyson lived at *Warninglid* for a year after his marriage, moved away but returned late in life (*Blackdown*). The painter Sir Oswald Birley owned a historic house at *Charleston* and inaugurated an annual Festival there. In our own day, the former Prime Minister Harold Macmillan, worthily created an earl in 1984, lives on the edge of Ashdown Forest, while celebrities of the entertainment world have homes in Sussex almost in their hundreds, attracted by the combination of the charm of countryside and coast with the virtue of easy access to London.

The ordinary people of Sussex deserve, and shall have, the last paragraph to themselves. 'Silly Sussex' (see *Selsey*) does not mean 'stupid Sussex' but happy or holy Sussex. Sussex people are proud when people who know the true meaning call them silly. Though they may be reluctant to be 'druv', they are happy and extremely open-hearted. Rare indeed have been the rebuffs we have met. Even in these days of threatened and often actual theft and vandalism, few church doors have failed to open. (It is a pity that when they were locked, doubtless for good reason, there was hardly ever a notice saying where the key might be obtained.) On every side we have met helpful friendliness. We hope that the scores of folk we have 'chatted up' will accept this expression of our gratitude.

Warden Swinfen
March 1984.

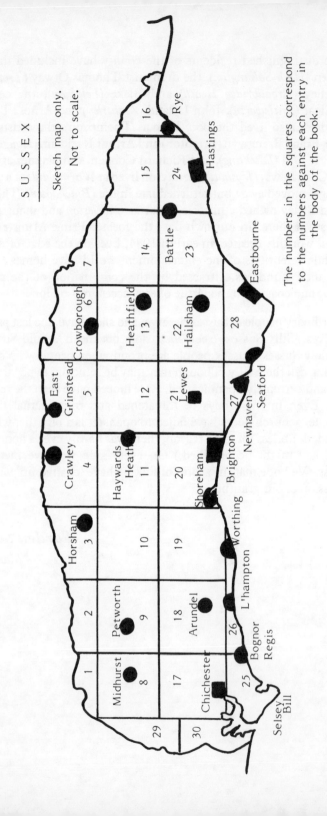

S U S S E X

Sketch map only.
Not to scale.

The numbers in the squares correspond
to the numbers against each entry in
the body of the book.

14

ADVERSANE

Let's begin by travelling the Roman way, for a short stretch at least. Adversane is little more than a cross-roads a couple of miles south of Billingshurst but the north-south A29 follows exactly the line of the great Stane Street from London down to Chichester (the Roman Noviomagus). It curved below Pulborough to take in a fortified 'mansion' or posting-station at Hardham, where travellers could change or water their horses and stay overnight. The line can then be traced to the villa at *Bignor,* down through *Halnaker* and Westhampnett into Chichester — but Adversane is the best place to grasp the relationship of the old road to the modern.

There were three roads coming down from London into Sussex in Roman times. Stane Street was primarily a military route, though traders would of course have used it. The road to Brighton branched from it in the Kennington area and came down via *Selsfield Common,* Haywards Heath, Burgess Hill and *Hassocks.* The London to Lewes way was first and foremost an industrial road, linking the corn-growing area of the South Downs to the capital and providing outlets for Wealden iron to the ports and naval establishments on the coast. Small parts of it can be seen at Camp Hill on Ashdown Forest, by the car park, and at *Holtye.*   [10]

ALBOURNE

A short way down Church Lane is the humble and elderly Spring Cottage, whose brick patchwork testifies to a great many additions and repairs. An inscribed stone tablet set in the wall facing the lane reads, none too grammatically:

> The Tenants of this
> Manour has Right
> to Fetch Water
> At this Spring
> MDCCXXXVI

Was this a response to a wrangle over the water-supply?

The inventor of the penny-farthing bicycle, James Starley, is said to have had private tuition in this cottage. The story goes that he sold machines to Queen Victoria after a publicity stunt in which he overtook her horse-drawn carriage by sheer pedal-power.

Further down the lane is the Old School House, now privately owned but with the original improving text cut in the stone around its door: 'The fear of the Lord is the beginning of wisdom'. The vestiges of an ancient watermill can be seen as 'humps and bumps' in the field opposite. A pair of parallel banks seems to have been constructed to divert Cutlers Brook.   [20]

15

ALCISTON

The largest tithe barn in the county, it's claimed, stands as part of Alciston Court. It's flint built with a steeply pitched tiled roof, and there are two pairs of double doors, one with a gabled porch, and an extension at right angles at one end. The total length is about 170 feet. It was originally a storage barn belonging to Battle Abbey, nearly twenty miles away.

Nearby, the church stands isolated on a hillock, and between church and barn is a ruined building rather like a giant's waffle-toaster. It is, or was, a medieval dovecote: what you see are the nesting-holes. Pigeons formed an important item of diet in the Middle Ages, and most monasteries and manor houses kept them in hundreds.

Alciston is one of a series of quaint villages tucked away under the north side of the Downs — most of them, including Firle, Folkington and Berwick, are at the ends of culs-de-sac.   [22]

ALDINGBOURNE

Turning off the A2024 (signpost 'Oving'), skirt Aldingbourne village, leaving the church on your right: a little further, in a field to your left, is a hump called 'Castle Mound'. Excavations here in the 1960's revealed remains of a Norman (later twelfth century) watch tower with surrounding walls and a moat. It was demolished in 1642, during the civil war, by Roundhead troops under Sir William Waller. After excavation it was covered over for preservation, forming the mound.

The church is patchy in interest; it has some medieval wall-painting, and Norman decoration on the chancel arch, but was much ruined by the Victorians.   [17]

ALDRINGTON

The only place where we found a fractional population! Mark Antony Lower, in his 'History of Sussex' tells us that there was once a tollgate on the road, a little east of where the lagoon is now. He wrote: 'According to the 1831 census, the population of the parish was two only — the toll-gate keeper and his wife. The poor man, who had lost a leg, also afterwards lost his partner, so that taking into account his physical deficiency, the actual population of Aldrington was but three-quarters of an inhabitant!'

Nowadays it's only a part of western Hove, and has no clear boundary. Along the seafront it extends roughly between the Sackville Hotel and Boundary Road, Portslade. Its name belongs principally to the basin overshadowed by the great power station. A stroll round the basin is quite an experience.   [20]

16

ALDSWORTH

The dominating feature of the village is Racton Tower, about half a mile to the north-east, on the summit of a hill. This typical eighteenth century folly stands gauntly above the church (for which see *Racton*). It was built in 1772 by Theodosius Keene for the third Earl of Halifax, whose seat was at Stansted Park, and it is said to have cost £10,000. Triangular in plan, it had a small tower at each corner and a much larger one in the centre. It was a favourite look-out place of the Earl's, and the story goes that he would invite local Excisemen to have a drink with him. Then, when he had got them thoroughly fuddled, he would wave flares from the top of the tower to indicate to nearby smugglers that the coast was clear!   [30]

ALDWICK

Amid a flurry of homes of varying degrees of opulence, and dating from the 1930s and later, a genuine old cottage makes an entrancing effect. Rose Cottage, on the corner of Rose Green Road, is thatched and whitewashed, and has dormer windows. But was it originally three cottages? The pattern of alternating dormers and below-eaves windows makes this seem at least possible. Further west, along the coast, was Craigweil House, where the convalescence of King George V in 1928 after serious illness brought Bognor its 'Regis' (see *Pagham*). Craigweil was demolished some years ago.   [26]

17

ALFRISTON

A local butcher, Stanton Collins, was transported in 1831 for receiving stolen bushels of barley, but you only have to tour his house to credit the strong local tradition that he led a smuggling gang. There are six staircases in this strange building (now the Smugglers Inn) and many of the rooms have a confusing choice of exits. One of them has no fewer than five doors!

There are plenty of good things in Alfriston. The market cross is now a mere stump, but is nevertheless one of only two survivors in Sussex, the other being at Chichester. The clergy house is a timber-framed and thatched house by the Tye, with the distinction of being the first building acquired by the National Trust. That was back in 1896, and it cost £10.

The church has associations with St. Lewinna, a virgin martyr killed by a heathen Saxon, about 680 A.D. Her remains were interred in a church dedicated to St. Andrew (as is Alfriston's), and many miracles were performed at her tomb. The bones of the saint were eventually stolen and taken to Flanders.   [28]

AMBERLEY

Amberley Wild Brooks inspired one of the best-known and loveliest piano pieces by John Ireland, who lived near here for many years. To reach them, go down the track north of the church and around the castle: ahead, across the fields, is the River Arun. Above you is the most awe-inspiring view of Amberley Castle (not open to the public). This was for nearly 400 years one of three county residences of the bishops of Chichester — the others were at Aldingbourne and Cakeham. It stands on ground recorded as having been given to St. Wilfrid in AD 681. The present castle was begun about AD 1100 by Bishop Luffa of Chichester, who was responsible also for starting the building of Chichester Cathedral.

For such a picturesque county, Sussex is somewhat short of truly picturesque villages. Many of them are pleasant but not captivating. Amberley, full of thatched cottages and narrow flower-decked pathways, is definitely captivating.   [18]

AMBERSTONE

Many toll houses survive in Sussex, but the one on the south side of the A271 at Amberstone is still almost as it was originally built (for the Battle-Broyle Park Gate turnpike) in 1776. Note the small observation windows at the side.   [22]

18

ANGMERING

Angmering-on-Sea is south of the A27, Angmering proper is north of it. St. Margaret's church is an exuberant piece of Victoriana giving no clue what the twelfth century original must have looked like — only the 1507 tower survives unharmed. The village's other church, St. Nicholas, just across the road, has vanished, to be replaced by St. Nicholas' Garden, provided by Angmering Parish Council. It was opened by Lavinia, Duchess of Norfolk, on May 8, 1980, and when we went it was looking rather neglected and sad. It contains a piece of stonework which is in fact a sculpture, though it suggests — perhaps intentionally — a remnant from the former building.   [26]

APPLEDRAM

The church has an organ whose history goes back directly to the Prince Consort. It was originally made for Albert about 1845 and was destined for Windsor Castle. Somehow it got diverted to Littlehampton, of all unlikely places, and then came here. The guidebook of the church refers you to several interesting graffiti, but there are more. On the north-west corner buttress are masons' marks like yachts, and on the outside jamb of the east window of the porch is a scratched design of a slender steeple — could it be Chichester cathedral's? Behind the pulpit are the remains of the staircase to the former rood-loft (see *Introduction*).

The Ryman family were landowners here in the fifteenth century and built a charming manor house south-east of the church. Originally it had a central tall tower with two wings at right angles, but one wing has gone. The story goes that Ryman imported his stone from France; the Bishop of Chichester had some of it diverted to build the bell-tower of the cathedral, once known as Ryman's tower.   [25]

ARDINGLY

College Road is truly named, for down it lies world-famous Ardingly College, one of the great boys' public schools — the buildings make an imposing group. Some 200 yards further on, down an unsignposted turning on the right, is the new Mid-Sussex reservoir. The authority have done it proud — splendid boating and fishing facilities, car parks, picnic areas, stunning views: everything for a day out.

North of the village centre is the South of England Show Ground, used for a variety of fairs, rallies and the like as well as for the big event in June, when farmers, stockbreeders and suppliers gather to look, talk and learn.   [11/12]

ARLINGTON

One of the most interesting churches in the county, with specimens of all architectural periods from Saxon onwards. Its contents include a large food storage jar (mid-thirteenth century in date), kept under glass in the north chapel, and a wooden chest whose boards are rough-cut from the tree. In several places can be seen fragments of the medieval painting which once doubtless covered the walls. The font-cover is fairly recent, but is of an interesting design and was made by a master blacksmith in the village.

Abbot's Wood, in the parish, existed at least as early as the time of Henry I (1100-1135), when it was owned by Battle Abbey. After the Dissolution it was transferred to the Gage family, but now it's managed by the Forestry Commission, with nature trails and other amenities. It is well sign-posted.   [22]

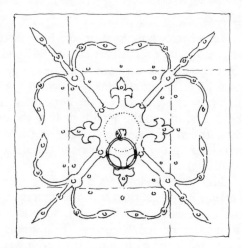

ASHBURNHAM

There are two relics of the Sussex industrial past in this village. On the north side of the minor road from Penhurst to Ponts Green are the double kiln, covered firing area and outbuildings of a former brickworks. It was the last wood-fired kiln in Sussex and was working until 1968. On a track north from Ashburnham Forge on the same road is the last iron furnace to be worked in the county. It dates from perhaps the seventeenth century and closed down in 1820. The masonry wheelpit can be found in the undergrowth, one of the few remaining stone relics of the iron industry in Sussex.

You can see three late eighteenth century stone mileposts on the line of a disused private carriage road from Ashburnham Place to the Flimwell-Hastings turnpike. The last of them, marked '55 miles from London — 2 miles to Ashburnham Place' is on a bank beside the old coach road, now a forest track.   [23]

ASHINGTON

At the far end of Church Lane, beyond the church, stands a delightful farmstead, part timbered, part brick, part tile-hung. Beside it is a tall, narrow barn with boarded sides and hipped roof. It immediately suggests a mill — which it originally was.

Alongside the church porch are two miniature gravestones whose inscriptions are now illegible. They are so tiny that they must surely have been for infants. At the other extreme is a twelve-feet high stone cross almost due west of the church. It carries long biblical texts and nothing more.   [19]

ASHLING

There are two: East and West. West is the more secluded and more attractive. 'Graingers' is a timbered cottage, and it and the barn next door have roofs mostly tiled which unexpectedly sprout thatch over the roof ridge and down the back. Another equally attractive house is called The Thatched House, and has brick nogging. Several cottages have overhanging upper floors, which increase the period sense. At the road junction is a cottage (with a letter box outside) which has not one, but two, fire-marks on the side wall.
     [17]

ASHURST

A vamphorn is a rarity these days — there are only half-a-dozen of them in the whole country, and one is in Ashurst church. It was a musical instrument used to give the pitch for singers, though we've seen it described as a kind of megaphone. Michael Fairless (Margaret Fairless Dowson), author of that delightful book 'The Road Mender', who died aged only 33, is buried in the churchyard.

The Fountain Inn, praised by Hilaire Belloc in 'The Four Men', dates in part from the sixteenth century; opposite it is a picturesque group of farm buildings.   [10]

ASHURSTWOOD

'Dutton Homestall' is a remarkable house, now a stud. It was in the fourteenth century a hunting lodge belonging to no less a person than John of Gaunt. It was then called 'Homestall'; but in 1933 it was much restored, and Dutton Hall was transported all the way from Cheshire and added on.   [5]

BALCOMBE

A chalybeate spring — that is, one rich in iron — rises in a wood to the north of the village. The surrounding vegetation is rust-coloured and the water (said to be beneficial because of its mineral content) leaves a taste in the mouth long after you've sipped it. Follow the marked footpath from the end of the attractive cul-de-sac at the village centre: the spring is surrounded by a fence at the foot of a steep flight of wooden steps.

On a completely different scale, the Ouse Valley railway viaduct is one of the wonders of Sussex. Built between 1839 and 1841, it stretches for nearly 500 yards and is almost 100 feet high with 37 arches. The materials for its construction were brought by barge up the river, and you can still find the semicircular turning bay, now choked by weeds, near Upper Rylands bridge. Ironically, the railway brought about the death of the Ouse Navigation.   [4]

BALDSLOW

Moving a vast statue of Queen Anne from London to Sussex in Victorian times must have been quite a job! She, with attendant figures of Britannia, Ireland, France and America at her feet, once occupied a place of honour in front of St. Paul's cathedral. The monarch had been carved by the distinguished sculptor Francis Bird, but by Victorian times she was becoming weather-worn, and she was ousted by a replica. The original was found discarded in a stonemason's yard in Southwark, by Augustus Hare, much-travelled author of topographical books including perhaps the first general guide to Sussex (1896). He brought it down to his country mansion, Holmhurst — now a convent, where it stands in the garden. You can see the statue from the road, or ask permission to enter from the nuns — inquire at the main entrance, in the side road to the north.   [24]

BARCOMBE

On the bridle-road approach to Barcombe House, above and below Pike's Bridge, are the two lock-chambers of the Upper Ouse Navigation. The locks have been adapted as weirs, and the navigation is a fish ladder, owned by the Southern Water Authority. A part of the parish known as Barcombe Mills was named for groups of mills often painted by artists until they were destroyed by fire in 1939. According to Domesday, in 1086 there were 3½ mills here, and later records prove a remarkable continuity, thanks to the river. A plaque on the road bridge records that here was the first tollgate in Sussex (1066).

Barcombe and Barcombe Mills had separate railway stations, both of which can be seen though the trains no longer run. You can walk along the disused track here. It's an excellent place for a family outing — as long as toddlers are kept from the water's edge!   [21]

BARGHAM

How many ways can you spell a name? In 1383 a lawsuit was tried in which Bargham was so spelt, but a little later it was the seat of a prebend under the name 'Bargeham'. Somehow it became 'Barpham', in which form it is found on some old maps and on the modern Ordnance Survey. In 1582 it's recorded as 'Barffham', and 'Bergham' and 'Bercam' are also known. Pevsner in 1965 still knows it as Bargham.

The medieval church, up on the Downs a couple of miles north of Angmering, was demolished about 1500. The remaining foundations were excavated and marked out in 1950. It's worth a visit for its remoteness and for the view.   [18]

BARLAVINGTON

Modern sculpture is not too common in our churches, but here is an expressive Annunciation, in wood with gilding, above the altar. In the churchyard, which adjoins a fully-operational farm, the tomb of Mr. and Mrs. Robert Foard has nice gothic cast-iron rails in trefoil design, with crocketed finials. Was Barlavington so remote that they were overlooked during the last war and so never taken for scrap?

There are several Lavingtons near here: the suffix -ington signifies a farm, and this one once belonged to Beornlaf. The farm you see now is equipped with much more modern plant. Surprisingly, this stretch of Downs is not rich in prehistoric remains, though the Roman villa at Bignor lies just below you.
                                                                          [9]

BARNHAM

Beside the Murrell Arms, at the entrance to Church Lane, is a small triangle of grass with three objects worth notice. First, a purple fig tree, planted in 1964 (says the plaque on a stone at its base) and now over twenty feet high; second, a sign directing you to the church, and commemorating the royal wedding on July 29, 1981 ('Lady Diana Spencer is descended from Charles, 5th Duke of Richmond 1791-1860, who owned a large part of this village. The Manor of Barnham was sold in 1776 to the 3rd Duke of Richmond.'); third, a rough stone pillar about three feet high, looking like a birdbath. It's the old pinnacle from Chichester Market Cross, A.D. 1501, and is 'to commemorate the liberation of the Falkland Islands, 14 June 1982'.

There's a mill at Barnham to which there is more than meets the eye. The remains comprise only the tower and cap, but wind power has given way to electrical. There is still a thriving milling business here: in fact, until a few years ago the original millstones were still being used.   [18]

BARNS GREEN

Blacksmith's Cottage is a charming reminder of how, long after the old use of a building has ceased to exist, a former owner's trade is borne into history. Many such homes still carry these occupational names, like 'Saddler's Cottage'. An idea for young passengers in your car — how many can you spot?   [10]

BATTLE

In the fields just a few minutes' walk from the ruins of Battle Abbey are the remnants of the gunpowder industry which thrived here from 1676 to 1874, when the Duke and Duchess of Cleveland, the then occupants of the Battle Abbey Estate, refused to renew the lease because of the danger of explosions. The mills had been among the largest in England. There are several large ponds in the area, created to give the industry its water-power, and in the grounds of the large country house close by are the remains of an 80 ft. tower. You can also spot remnants of some of the workshops, while the powder packing house and the blacksmith's forge are now private residences.

The Battle of Hastings was fought here on October 14, 1066, and victorious William vowed to build an abbey on the site almost immediately after, the altar being positioned on the exact spot where Harold fell. The abbey gateway faces the main square; the ruins are generally open through the summer. In the square a brass plate marks the place where bulls were tethered for the bull-baiting — a sport for which the town was famous.

On the north wall of the church is a memorial to Edmund Cartwright, the inventor of the power loom, while in the graveyard is the tomb of Isaac Ingall, who died in 1798 aged 120, and who was butler at the Abbey for 95 years.

[23/24]

24

BAYHAM

The ruins of Bayham Abbey are the most splendid in the county — comparable with many in Yorkshire. One wall of the nave is largely standing, while the chancel, clearly outlined and with a slab marking the site of the high altar, has been invaded by a large tree. The north transept is not only standing but roofed, and the details of the carving on the capitals are very fine and will repay close inspection. Pevsner explains clearly the sequence of building, and the official guide is readable and thorough. The whole site is now in the care of the Department of the Environment, who are excavating it with their usual care and devotion, and looking after it very well. Sussex, incidentally, is *not* a county where the D. of E. are very active.

As usual in medieval monasteries, Bayham Abbey has a separate gatehouse away to the north-west. This stands on the very edge of a stream, with the more modern Bayham Abbey house on the other side. But that's in Kent — the county boundary runs along the bed of the stream, called the Teise: it's a tributary of the Medway, and is dammed to form a lake a bit further west.   [7]

BECKLEY

The 'dug out chest' is something to look out for in the church. It's thought to be twelfth century and has on it some of the earliest ironwork in the county. Scored and pitted, the chest was dug out of a single tree-trunk. The rector and the wardens would each have held a different key, and the chest could only be opened when all three were present — a system still used by some financial institutions today.   [15]

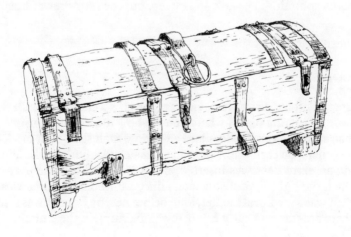

BEDDINGHAM

The most prominent landmark in central Sussex is the spur of Mount Caburn, round which the A27 road east of Lewes curves towards Firle. The best access to the top of the hill starts in Glynde village, where almost opposite the entrance to Glynde Place starts a path marked 'Licensed footpath to Mount Caburn'. On the summit of the mount (height nearly 500 feet) is a small and well-investigated Iron Age hill-fort consisting of a massive outer rampart and ditch and a smaller inner pair. More than 140 grain storage pits dating from the first centuries B.C. have been located and can still be traced as hollows in the ground.

Although Curwen's 'Archaeology of Sussex' is in some respects out of date, one can hardly quarrel with his estimate that the population of the fort was around 200 to 300, that springs and surface water were relied upon, and that the inhabitants made goods of bronze, iron and other materials which they could trade or barter for the other necessities of life.

The view from here is superb, the River Ouse and Glynde Reach curling away beneath you. [21]

BEPTON

At Linch Farm, half a mile west of the village, there is in one corner of a field, a stout brick tower, just by the roadside towards Didling. It can hardly be either a water-tower or a mill, and we think it's another eighteenth century folly, placed in a prominent position to look romantic. It is now used for farm purposes. Bepton church, in the village, has vast brick angle-buttresses, and from here there is a fine view across to Bepton Down, with a good group of tumuli on its summit. The walk up is steep, but the result rewarding. [8]

BERSTED

Vicarage Cottage never was a vicarage, but it's a charmer for all that. It's one of those intriguing places where you see how it grew. The original stone cottage had simply a central door and a window each side, with brick quoins (edges or corners) on each wall. Then an extension was built on the left, still of stone, and an extra door was inserted, now disused. Then there was a flint extension on the right — probably later, since a different material was used.

Bersted was a medieval hamlet, long before nearby Bognor was starting to grow. There are traces of early English wall-painting in the church. [18/26]

BERWICK

The wall paintings in the church are a reminder that the medieval congregation would have been surrounded by bright illustrations, designed for their moral edification. These, however, are twentieth century works, painted during the second world war by three of the Bloomsbury group — Duncan Grant, Vanessa Bell and her son Quentin Bell. Note the Sussex features, including the well-laden trug basket in the Nativity. And the angels above the chancel arch have impeccable Forties hair-do's.   [28]

BIGNOR

On July 18, 1811, a farmer named George Tupper felt his plough strike a stone. Moving the stone, he found part of the now celebrated 'Ganymede' mosaic of what proved to be the remains of a very large Roman villa of the early second century A.D. Numerous excavations over the years have uncovered many superb mosaic floors, and it has been possible to reconstruct the complete plan. In the north corridor is the longest continuous mosaic to be seen anywhere — eighty-two feet of it. Here, too, are the famous 'Venus and the Gladiators' and 'The Four Seasons' — the lady symbolising Winter looking thoroughly frozen. Mosaic is an art whose beauty and intricacy become clearer the longer you look at it, and these examples are quite outstanding.

Stane Street (see *Adversane*) ran about half a mile east, and a branch road served the villa itself. It ran up a spur of the neighbouring Down, on whose summit the causeway itself is visible between ditches.

Models and plans in the excellent on-site museum will help you to follow the whole layout.   [18]

BILLINGSHURST

Almost too big to be classed as a village, Billingshurst has a classic example of a lopsided church. Seen from the west, the roof is way off-centre, the south side having a much steeper slope than the north, while the tower buttresses are equally ill-matched: a huge clasping buttress to the south-west, two much smaller angle ones on the north-west. The explanation must lie in restoration work. The Tudor porch is typical of its period, and a good example to boot. Inside the church, there is a panelled ceiling and a late fifteenth century brass of no special distinction.

The sixteenth century Olde Six Bells Inn, just opposite, is a real charmer.

[10]

BINDERTON

Hardly even a hamlet, just a small group of houses on the road between Midhurst and Chichester, grouped around an ivy-clad ruin. Yet it testifies to one of Sussex's oddest stories, delightfully told in the local church guide-book. An autocrat named Thomas Smith, who lived across the road, had the old church demolished during the 1650s, and a new one built just east of what is now the A286 road. Neither action had any lawful authority, and the new church was never consecrated. When Mr. Smith came to make his will, he required his body to be buried in his new church even if it had not been sanctified. Upon his death six Anglican clergymen acted as pall-bearers, but when they reached the church door they refused to go further since the ground was unhallowed. To put things right, a Presbyterian father was sent for post-haste, and he preached over Smith's coffin the only sermon ever delivered in the building. We confess that the thought of six august Anglican priests 'downing tools', as it were, and going on strike at the very door of the church appealed to our sense of humour.

The church ruin is still standing right by the roadside. It was used for years as a farm building, until it fell into disrepair; but the outline of one of two churchly window-frames can still be seen. [17]

BINES GREEN

A tiny hamlet slightly north of Ashurst. Ian Nairn described it as 'one of the best places in this part of Sussex to see the whole repertoire of cottage building'. Almost any cottage is a joy, but Martinsland Farm, at the north end, is one of the most charming farmhouse groups anywhere in Sussex.[10]

BINSTED

A rather spread-out group of houses including, just off the B2132, the charming 'Beam Ends', and opposite it 'Old School Laundry House' — a house-name to conjure with!

The church is right through the village, and though small has two interesting points. The chancel pavement is nineteenth century, but makes use of a technique originating in twelfth century Italy — the 'Cosmati' patterns. Also, the Victorian 'restoration' involved raising the sanctuary, so that now the piscina (a small stone basin used for washing the sacred vessels at Mass) is oddly situated about 18 inches off the floor.   [26]

BIRDHAM

A mill at Birdham is mentioned in Domesday but the motive power is unclear. Part of the parish was once known as East Itchenor, which is why modern Itchenor is technically West Itchenor. The picturesque Old Mill is a tidal mill built on the edge of Chichester harbour in 1768, and by 1925 was the last such mill still in working order. The nearby Mill House is dated 1780. The mill is now the headquarters of the local yacht club.

A little north of the village is the western end of the Chichester Canal, and alongside is the Chichester Yacht Basin. Saltern's Lock, beside the basin, is the sole remaining working lock on the canal, and at eight feet depth is capable of taking seagoing vessels. It is nowadays used solely by pleasure boats. [25]

BIRLING

Birling was once a manor place, which later became a farmhouse and is still called Birling Farm. It stands near the head of Birling Gap, a hollow in the final ridge of the South Downs before they rise to their easternmost climax at Beachy Head. Smuggling stories in Sussex are legion, and there are few we would go to the stake for, but there's no doubt that a great deal of contraband found its way ashore here.

M. A. Lower's 'History of Sussex' (1870) records that at Birling Gap 'is the junction of the submarine and inland telegraph from Paris to London via Dieppe'. West of Birling Gap are the Seven Sisters, undulating chalk cliffs. Many people don't realise that the Sisters all have names, so it's a pleasure to record them. From west to east they are called Haven Brow (or Cliff End), Short Brow, Rough Brow, Brass Point, Flagstaff Point, Bailey's Brow and Went Hill Brow. East of Went Brow and the road from East Dean is the old disused Belle Tout lighthouse (see *East Dean*).   [28]

BISHOPSTONE

One of the earliest churches in the whole county, with part surviving from the early eighth century. As you enter the church porch the first thing you notice is that the inner door is well off-centre. It is in this unbalanced position because in early days there would have been an altar on the east wall of the porch itself: there is a niche for a cross or statue. At weddings the priest would meet the couple at the church door and ask them if they were willing to be joined in matrimony. If they were, they would take vows at the porch altar before entering the church to complete the ceremony. Various contracts used to be solemnised in this way, if they were important enough to justify the making of a sworn vow.

Over the porch entrance is a sundial, up in the gable, inscribed EADRIC. The name was common in Saxon times, and may be that of the donor. Sundials were common on churches to indicate the times of services: in this case the radiating lines indicate hours, the longer crossed lines being for the main three-hourly Saxon 'tides'. There was a gnomon projecting from the centre hole, but to find one surviving nowadays is a rarity indeed. [27]

BLACKBOYS

Nothing to do with our coloured population — the name means either 'Black Wood' or 'Blake's Wood': there is a record of a Richard Blakeboy in 1397/98. It's a small village with an historic pub called (not surprisingly) 'The Blackboys Inn', which dates from the fourteenth century and was clearly a posting stage for coaches travelling from London through Uckfield to Hastings. On the opposite side of the now residential road beside the inn is a group of cottages which look like converted stables. [13]

BLACKDOWN

Here on the greensand is the highest point in Sussex, at 919 feet higher than any point on the South Downs. On the slope of the hill, in 1868, Tennyson began the building of his second home, and he lived here until his death in 1892. He was already Poet Laureate (since 1850) and was made a peer in 1884. (See also *Warninglid*). His home, Aldworth House, almost on the Surrey border, still stands. [1]

BOARSHEAD

A group of cottages a few hundred yards towards Eridge from the Boars Head pub (a handsome medieval building) is a reminder that even the smallest hamlet once had its industrial centre. The forge and the wheelwright's and carpenter's shops are now private homes, but the forge, despite its new brickwork, is worth a respectful glance. Jack Fenner, the third in a line of smiths, worked here until his death in 1979 at the age of 92. It's thought that he was the last maker of handmade edge-tools in England.

Just up from the pub, on the other side of the road, is a pond which locals will tell you is the deepest in Sussex. We can't verify that, but we do know that it's well supplied even in the driest weather. [6]

BODIAM

The picture-book castle within its moat is the best-known feature of the village. It was started in 1385, a few years after Rye and *Winchelsea* had been badly mauled by the French, but by the time it was completed the English had regained control of the Channel and no battle was ever fought here. The castle (now little more than a shell) is owned by the National Trust and is open to the public during the season. You enter through a gatehouse armed with an impressive array of defensive features, including 'murder holes' in the ceiling through which missiles would have been hurled onto the heads of attackers. It's one of the last medieval castles: there are gunports for the cannon which, through their destructive power, were to render these traditional fortifications obsolete. Like many of its kind it fell into sad decay, only to be rescued by George Cubitt MP (afterwards Lord Ashcombe), son of Thomas Cubitt the builder responsible for much of Brighton. He sold it in 1917 to the Marquis Curzon of Kedleston who brought it up to the glory it is now.

Railway enthusiasts will wish to make a pilgrimage to the now disused Bodiam station, a humble building painted cream and maroon with a rusting loco as its only companion. There are plans to extend the Kent and East Sussex Railway towards Northiam and Bodiam. One of the six bells of St. Giles church is named after Haile Selassie: a previous rector was the Ethiopian emperor's aide-de-camp. [15]

BODLE STREET

Along the minor road to Dallington — and this area is a labyrinth of winding lanes — look out for Redpale Farmhouse, reputedly the home of one of Henry the Eighth's tutors. There's certainly no doubting its age, part of the frontage looking just as it must have done in the sixteenth century. There's an ancient barn, too. Less venerable, but still a comparative rarity, is the Victorian letterbox set into the garden wall.   [23]

BOLNEY

The churchyard has one special feature, all too rare these days — a full-blown lych-gate. 'Lych' is an old English word for a corpse, and originally when a coffin was brought to the church for burial, it would rest under a covered gate at the entrance to the hallowed ground until the priest came to meet it and conduct the first part of the funeral service. This lych-gate is complete with central stone table on which the coffin could be rested, and there is access on both sides for the bearers.

Although the gate is modern, it's entirely made of traditional Sussex materials: oak timbers, Sussex marble, and a pair of local millstones. It was given to the church in 1905 by Mr. Edward Huth, of whose family there are several memorials inside the church. Henry Huth, an earlier member of the family, commissioned 'Wykehurst' (1872-4), a house standing off the A23, which looks just like a decayed French château and has been used on several occasions as a setting for macabre films.   [11]

BOREHAM STREET

Boreham Street Farm has a good barn, and next to it an oast house in good condition. Oast houses, almost entirely confined to Kent and East Sussex, are used for drying the hops used in brewing.

Round oast houses with a vane on the rotatable funnel-top, to turn with the wind, were introduced in the early nineteenth century, and sometimes you find groups of them (see *Udimore*), built when the brewing industry enjoyed its greatest boom. Hop plants are grown up long strings, and until the 1950s hop-picking by hand was a regular holiday activity for thousands of Londoners, until machines took over. Many oasts have been turned into attractive and unusual living rooms of private homes.   [23]

32

BOSHAM

The Saxon cornerstones of the sturdy church are the ones depicted in the Bayeux tapestry scene in which Harold kneels to pray before the trip to Normandy in 1064 which led to his eventual downfall at Hastings. By tradition the building is much older than that. The Venerable Bede, writing about 730 AD, recorded that a seventh century Irish monk named Dicul had 'a very small monastery in a place which is called Bosanham, a spot surrounded by woods and the sea'.

Bosham is one of the three important Saxon churches in Sussex, and the strength of the tower and chancel arches are typical of Saxon building. Yet it comes as a surprise that no Hundred of Bosham is mentioned in Domesday: the reason is that it was then a royal manor. Among several interesting features in the church are an unusual crypt, now dedicated to Dicul, but much later in date and probably a bone-house; and the grave of one of King Canute's daughters, who name has not come down to us. Tradition had claimed that the child was buried in the church but no evidence existed until in August 1865 the Rev. H. Mitchell directed masons to sound the spot and a coffin containing the body of a child of about 8 years old was uncovered. The present slab, bearing the raven of the Danish royal house, was given by the children of the village in 1906.   **[17/30]**

BOTOLPHS

Botolph, who died in 680, was an East Anglian abbot whose relics were regarded with special veneration in medieval times. His church, near Bramber, served a village now forsaken. The railway line (now disused and so overgrown as to be scarcely distinguishable) passed right next to the churchyard, in which is planted a tree to commemorate the Queen's Jubilee in 1977. Inside the church is quite a bit of Saxon work, to remind us of its venerable antiquity.   **[19/20]**

BOXGROVE

In the Priory church is the only complete chantry chapel remaining in all Sussex. Chantries were endowed for the saying of masses for the souls of the founder and his family — in this case Lord de la Warr, who died in 1526.

Masses for the dead ceased with the Reformation, and many chapels were barbarously defaced. This chapel, almost like a little church in itself, is ornately carved with grotesque monsters and nude men in the panels, a Dance of Death, a man climbing a tree on one pillar, and so on. The carver was clearly a fine craftsman, but where did he get his ideas from?

William Caxton established his printing press at Westminster in 1476, and soon printed books also began to be imported. Foreign booksellers set up shops in London, many in St. Paul's Churchyard. One was Simon de Vostre, whose Paris associates produced innumerable religious books with engraved illustrations — scenes from the Bible, 'portraits' of prophets and the like. Many of the delightful figures and scenes in this chapel are 'cribbed' directly from the engravings in these books.

The monastic buildings have largely disappeared; the chapter house door and the guest house are the principal survivals.   [17]

BRACKLESHAM

Here's the place to find sharks' teeth 60 million years old! The shore of the bay is renowned for fossils, which used to be found here in large numbers. The supply has diminished of late, perhaps due to a change in tidal currents, but you'll still find shells ages old washed about your feet.

At the time of the Armada, in 1588, a Spanish frigate, the Cartagena, was grounded in the bay. There's a persistent story that some of her timbers were abstracted for use in building Cartagena Farm, on the B2198 a mile or so north of Earnley. However, W. R. Read, in his little book on Birdham, tells us that the ship was towed away and repaired, and if that's true only a small quantity of timber can have been so used. It's a nice story, all the same.

The history of Bracklesham is largely one of coastal erosion. The coast strip was formerly (before 1518) an independent parish with its own chapel. By the early nineteenth century even the site seems to have been forgotten, and was probably well under the sea.

Ancient records show that in 945 King Edmund gave some land at Bracklesham to the then Bishop of Selsey, and in 1298 consent was given to the erection of a watermill on the existing mill pond. Nowadays the whole strip is devoted to modern bungalows and small houses.   [25]

BRAMBER

It's hard to believe, from the meagre watercourse running under Beeding bridge, that large boats once came up the broad river Adur as far as Bramber. Where the car park of the medieval house, St. Mary's, now lies there was a magnificent stone bridge, about 170 feet long and 17 feet wide, with four arches and a large chapel above the centre pier on the south side. Bramber was a centre for the Knights Templars, warrior monks later suppressed (see *Sompting*).

The ruins of Bramber Castle, built by the Normans on a hill above the village, are particularly recommended for energetic children. Little of the once-impressive walls remains, but the ground falls away steeply to a dry moat and there's a central mound, now tree-covered. The Normans relied on five great castles to defend Sussex from sea-raiders — the others being Hastings, Pevensey, Lewes and Arundel.

A good local story highlights the corrupt political practices of pre-Reform Bill times. William Wilberforce was an MP for the 'rotten borough' of Bramber (having outbid his rivals in cash for the few votes involved) and in 1819 he happened to pass through the town on his travels. Told where he was, he's said to have exclaimed: 'Bramber? This must be the place I'm Member for!'

There's a unique museum here, devoted entirely to smoking. It's called 'The House of Pipes', but it's much more than that, covering tobacco, matches, cigarette cards and packets, and many other things. [19]

BREDE

The parishioners of Brede would probably object to having their church compared with a museum: for one thing it's clearly well loved and used by the modern congregation. But there are similarities. The church houses a wealth of interesting features, all clearly labelled for the visitor. They include an ancient alms box of 1687, a pitch pipe, a seventeenth-century carved chest and the tomb of Sir Goddard Oxenbridge, 'the Brede giant', who was said to be seven feet tall. There are modern items, too, including a straw crucifix made by the natives of Oaxaca in Mexico (though how and why it came to Brede we aren't told). Outstanding is the madonna carved from the trunk of an oak by Clare Sheridan, the traveller, writer and artist: the tree was growing in the park at her home at Brede Place. Her own bust by Epstein is near the south aisle window opposite her madonna in the Lady Chapel. See also the Stations of the Cross by Sir Thomas Monnington, a former president of the Royal Academy.

Sir Goddard Oxenbridge was in reality a gentle person, but legends turned him from a giant into an ogre. He's supposed to have had a child roasted every day for his dinner, until the children of Sussex set a trap for him at Groaning Bridge. They brewed an especially potent kind of beer and put it out for him to drink. When he passed out from its effects, they laid a huge saw on him — the East Sussex children at one end, the West Sussex ones at the other — and sawed him in half! [24]

BRIGHTLING

The Brightling area bears the eccentric stamp of John (Mad Jack) Fuller, member of an ancient family of iron-founders who lived at Heathfield during the sixteenth and seventeenth centuries and who established the foundry at Waldron. John (1757-1834) was one of those men who attract legends — none of which we can guarantee — but it's clear that he was, in fact, far from mad. He commissioned the artist Turner to paint local scenes; the architect Sir Robert Smirke to design some of his buildings; and the landscaper Humphrey Repton to advise on the layout of his estates. He was a Member of Parliament for a long period.

His sobriquet derives largely from his delight in building follies and fancies, of which there are several in the area (see also *Dallington*). Turn north from the Heathfield-to-Battle road at Wood's Corner and you'll first pass the Observatory on your right. It's now a private house. The Needle, 40 feet high, was erected on Brightling Beacon 650 feet above sea level (and later used for signalling during the Napoleonic wars) and elsewhere there are a temple and a tower. Fuller, who devised several projects in order to alleviate unemployment, was buried under an 80 feet high pyramid in Brightling churchyard, and the story went that he was interred sitting at a table, a glass of port in one hand and a bottle at his side. Alas, when the mausoleum was opened in 1983 it was found to be empty, so that another colourful piece of local lore was proved baseless.

Among the many objects of interest in the church are the wall paintings and a barrel organ dating from 1820 — the largest in Britain in full working order. When it was installed, Fuller presented the male members of the choir with white smocks, buskin breeches and yellow stockings and the girls with red cloaks. [14]

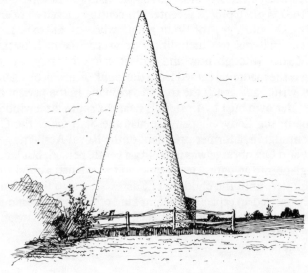

BROADBRIDGE HEATH

'Field Place', now a farm, lies a short distance north of the village, down a side road from the B2199 to Warnham. Parts of it are fifteenth century, but the tallest part dates from about 1678. It was the birthplace of the poet Shelley, whose forebears had lived and owned land in Sussex for generations. The poet left the house while still young, and became estranged from his father. In 1815 his grandfather, Sir Bysshe Shelley died. Shelley came back but was refused admission to the house, even to hear the reading of the will.   [3]

BROADWATER

One of the most splendid tombs in any parish church in the south of England is here. It's in the chancel, and is of Thomas West, Lord de la Warr, who died in 1524/5. A later generation of the family lies in the fine, though damaged, tomb in the south transept. Broadwater church is largely Norman and has close associations with the earldom of de la Warr. On the tomb in the chancel is an old tilting-helmet supposed to have belonged to the family, and originally hung as a trophy on Thomas's monument. Sometime in the eighteenth century it was converted into a poor-box and fixed in front of the former pulpit (which was replaced in 1866). Now it has returned in its proper guise to its proper place.

In the churchyard lie buried two naturalist authors: W. H. Hudson and Richard Jefferies. Though both travelled widely, they both remained true sons of Sussex. We can't resist quoting from Jefferies' 'The Life of the Fields' a passage which would surely have upset Dr. Russell:

> *"If the air at the sea-beach is good, that of the hills above the sea is at least twice as good, and twice as strengthening. It possesses all the virtue of the sea air without the moisture which ultimately loosens the joints, and seems to penetrate to the very nerves. Those who desire air and quick recovery should go to the hill, where the wind has a scent of the sunbeams."*

Broadwater is now a suburb north of Worthing, but it used to be a coastal village. Old maps often omit Worthing altogether. Broadwater was the parish church of the town until 1893, three years after Worthing became a borough.
                    [26]

BUCKS GREEN

The best houses in the village are all commercial. The Fox Inn is up on a slight incline, and all the better for it. Another pub, the Queen's Head is equally charming in a less flamboyant way. Goblin's Pool Restaurant, next door, is rather overdone but undeniably eye-catching.   [3]

BULVERHYTHE

Two fragments of the former parish church, both parts of the chancel north wall, still stand in Hythe Avenue. The parish survived after the church fell into ruin in the fifteenth century, until it was absorbed into St. Leonard's in the early 19th century. Yet, remarkably, the place-name still lives on. [24]

BUNCTON

A real piece of Hidden Sussex — it's quite difficult to find the little chapel behind its screen of trees. On the A283 about a mile east of Washington is a road leading northwards, almost opposite the track up to Chanctonbury Ring. A few hundred yards up this road, on the east, is a belt of trees which dip into a hollow and up again, and here is a small signpost to the chapel. It well repays the scramble, with its tall Norman dimensions, its fine interior woodwork, and a view across to the Downs. It was formerly a chapel-of-ease to Ashington.
[19]

BURPHAM

A long way down a cul-de-sac road, immediately south of the railway bridge beside Arundel station, but worth every inch of the way. The church stands proudly at a hilltop: on the south side is a long Danish 'promontory' fort, still clearly traceable, and entered between two grassy mounds. Outside and inside, the church is a joy for lovers of Norman architecture. Look particularly at the moulding around the arch leading into the south transept, and on the transept side. It has a chevron, or 'V', formation, typically Norman, which travels right round the arch. But it has been carved in three dimensions and looks for all the world as if a series of lengths of broomstick had been chamfered off and joined together. The only other recorded instance of this ornament that we know of is in a church at Ely.

Burpham offers a remarkable demonstration of the continuity of occupation of the area. The Danish fort lies halfway up the Arun Gap, commanding the course of the navigable river. And there in the distance lies its successor, Arundel Castle. The Norman church lies between the two in date, and in the Middle Ages at Lee Farm was one of the two leper settlements in West Sussex (the other was in Chichester).

Keep your eyes open along the road running north-east from the village. A small cast-iron pump and horse basket stand close to one another beneath a cottage window. [18]

BURTON

Lady Elizabeth Goring, who died in 1588 (the year of the Spanish Armada) and is buried in Burton church, has a unique claim to fame. A brass on her tomb shows her wearing a tabard: it's the only brass in England showing a woman wearing this heraldic costume. The church stands in Burton Park, a little way east of the A285 and in delightful surroundings.

A little to the south is Burton Mill, another of those relics of rural industry which are now lovingly cared for by groups of enthusiasts. This is very much a working watermill regularly open to visitors through the summer months.

[9]

BURWASH

Half-way down the high street is an unusual ceramic map of the village, showing all the footpaths and manors within the parish. The work of local artist Eileen Ware, it was commissioned in memory of Judge Ellam and his wife by their daughter, who lives in America.

A badly defaced cast-iron slab on the wall of the church is in memory of 'Jhone Colins'. The lettering is said to be Lombardic, which suggests to some people a 14th century dating, but keen-witted scholars have pointed out that cast-iron wasn't made in Sussex until 1497 and grave slabs not until about 1550.

Batemans, now owned by the National Trust, was built by a local ironmaster and is celebrated for being the home of Rudyard Kipling: it's kept much as he left it. A watermill of 1750 in the grounds was adapted by the writer in 1903. He removed the water wheel and installed a turbine to drive a generator which supplied light to the house until the 1920s. It has recently been restored. **[14]**

BURY

The village stores and adjoining house are adorned with some most extraordinary carvings. They are, we imagine, nineteenth century, and depict such an odd assortment as a horse's head, a satyr, a green man, a seraph, and Puck sticking out his tongue. And there's a lady wearing an oakleaf coronet and biting something quite unmentionable.

Just down the road there is still a notice saying 'ferry closed'. It once took foot passengers across the river Arun to meet a path to Arundel, but so far as we know it hasn't operated for over half a century!

John Galsworthy, author of 'The Forsyte Saga', lived in Bury House. On its front is a plaque stating that 'John Galsworthy (1867-1933) — Author — lived the last seven years of his life in Bury House'. Very nice, too, though the 'Tudor' style of this gracious house dates from as recently as 1910. [18]

BUXTED

The funniest serious word in the English language must be a 'ha-ha'. It's a sunken wall in a ditch, originally designed to keep out cattle without obstructing the view. There's a fine specimen to be seen as you walk past the church in Buxted Park towards the main entrance to Buxted Park House — which is pretty spectacular in its own right.

The church is full of curiosities: in the chancel roof are two inverted plaster vases, while beside the north door is a wall-case containing old musical instruments and other treasures. Some of the ancient brasses have been remounted, and there is a bulky thirteenth century shrine chest, almost a unique piece. From the twentieth century comes a plaque remembering Basil Ionides (1884-1950), distinguished architect and designer of Buxted Park.

Hogge House dates from 1581. Ralph Hogge, ironmaster, reputedly cast the first cannon in England.   [13]

CADE STREET

At school most of us were taught about Jack Cade's rebellion of 1450. Cade, who claimed descent from the Mortimer family, raised an army of insurgents dissatisfied with political and living conditions. With Cade at their head, they marched on London, seized the Tower and beheaded the extortioner Lord Saye, the Treasurer. The rebellion was eventually put down. Cade himself was pursued and killed at Cade Street, where a memorial was set up saying: 'Near this spot was slain the notorious rebel Jack Cade, by Alexander Iden, Esq.'. E. V. Lucas, in 'Highways and Byways in Sussex', tells the whole story.   [13]

CAKEHAM

St. Richard is so much associated with Chichester that he almost escapes notice in our pages; but Cakeham manor house was from the 12th century a favourite residence of Bishops of Chichester, including Richard de Wyche, so we include him even more gladly because at least two of his miracles are connected with Cakeham. The remains of the present fifteenth century house are dominated by a remarkable pentagonal tower, the highest building for miles around, which changes its silhouette continuously as you go round it.   [25]

CAMBER

Camber boasts the only 'Henrican' castle in Sussex — that is, one built by Henry the Eighth — though it must be stressed that the remains are at some distance from the holiday settlement known as Camber Sands. After Henry broke with Rome there was a real danger of invasion, and he quickly set about defending the major ports and landing places. Camber Castle was erected on a peninsula of land jutting out into the sea in a good position to guard Rye bay. Now a mile of shingle separates the castle from the sea: you reach it along a footpath from the bridge on Rye harbour. With the retreat of the sea the castle lost its strategic position and it was dismantled in 1642. The Henrican forts were essentially elaborate gun-platforms, low and squat and designed to withstand enemy shot, but moats, drawbridges, portcullises and murder holes were also incorporated. There are plans for opening Camber to the public.[16]

CATSFIELD

George Stephenson, railway pioneer, did far more than build the 'Rocket'. With his partner Thomas Brassey, he laid railways in five continents. Brassey is buried in Catsfield churchyard — but the parish church is not the one with the lofty spire, which is Methodist. The parish church's south wall, west of the porch, has Norman stonework laid at crazy angles, without any apparent science at all.   [23]

CHAILEY

A little to the east of the church is Ades, the house purchased by Dr. Richard Russell of sea-bathing fame, which he left to his son Serjeant Kempe of Malling Deanery. But it's not the earliest recorded house here; that distinction belongs to 'The Hooke', south-west of the church. In 1317 William atte Hooke was charged with felony and his estates were seized for the king.

Chailey Common is traditionally the centre of Sussex. The exact site was always claimed to be at the yew tree beside Beards's Mill, which lies a short distance north-west of the junction of the A272 and A275 roads, across from the King's Head public house. This slim mill has been renovated and is worth inspecting.

Chailey's main claim to fame is the Heritage, an institution for crippled children founded in 1903 and so successful in its work that a New Heritage some distance away has had to be added to the original buildings designed by Comper.   [12]

CHALVINGTON

A kick from a a horse can be dangerous, a fact we tend to forget. But witness Job Guy, whose tombstone stands in the churchyard. He 'departed this life by a kick from a horse 17th April 1878, aged 8 years and 2 weeks'.

Sussex is not well endowed with ancient glass in its parish churches, but there is a small quantity here. The three pieces of arrowhead-shaped tracery in the east window contain an inscription in Lombardic lettering, to the effect that the then rector of the church Tho[ma]s Diliwyt had the window installed. Diliwyt held the living from 1388 to 1409, so the glass is datable to c.1400 AD.

High up in the gable at each end of the nave are small windows. In the seventeenth century a ceiling was sometimes inserted at eaves level in a church and such windows were provided to light the roof space.   [22]

CHANCTONBURY

Chanctonbury Ring is one of the county's best known sights. The name is given to the clump of trees planted by Charles Goring in 1760, when he was a mere 17 years old. The hill itself, which rises to nearly 800 feet, has long been of interest to archaeologists. On the summit are neolithic earthworks, inside which was built a Roman temple. Excavations have yielded stone-age flints, Roman coins and various items of pottery showing that the site was occupied for many centuries. There are several dewponds in the area (see *Introduction*). There is no village called Chanctonbury — the name belongs to the hill. [19]

CHARLESTON

Sir Oswald Birley, the painter (1880-1952) lived at Charleston Manor, and inaugurated an annual summer festival. There is a particularly fine dovecote in the garden. It's circular with a conical roof and its walls are about 2½ feet thick. It has no fewer than 350 nesting holes, and there is a ladder hinged centrally, so that it can be rotated to give access to all of them. The house itself is fascinating, with parts ranging from Norman to Georgian. The river Cuckmere passes quite close, and stumps of long-departed bridges can still be seen in the stream. There are some quite close to Charleston Manor.

A place with the same name, and also with painterly connections, is not to be confused with it. Charleston *Farmhouse* is on the Gage estate under Firle Beacon and was the home of 'Bloomsbury' artists Vanessa Bell and Duncan Grant (see *Berwick*). [21]

CHARLTON

Hunting in the eighteenth century was the sport of lords and ladies, and the Charlton Hunt was one of the most famous in the country. Fox Hall, which still exists, was built as a hunting lodge for the Duke of Richmond; the Duke's family still owns Goodwood House and much of the land in this area. Another Duke — of Devonshire — joined with Lord Harcourt in erecting a pair of hunting lodges. When the Hunt lost its fashionable importance the pair were converted into a single farmhouse. Now, fairly recently, re-conversion has made them a pair again. One of the huntsmen, Thomas Johnson, has a memorial in Singleton church. [17]

CHIDDINGLY

Frederick Harrison, in his 'Notes on Sussex Churches', written in the early years of this century, listed four churches in Sussex with ancient stone spires. One (East Preston) has gone, the other three remain, the oldest and finest being here at Chiddingly. It is early fifteenth century in date and soars 128 feet in height. Inside the church is a series of tombs of the Jefferay family, culminating in the stupendous alabaster monument to Sir John Jefferay, Baron of Exchequer under Elizabeth the First, in full legal robes.

At nearby Muddle's Green was born Mark Antony Lower, one of the most noteworthy sons of our county. He was a historian of Sussex, one of the founders of the Sussex Archaeological Society, and author of the fascinating 'Worthies of Sussex', besides much more. [22]

CHIDHAM

Bosham Channel is one of the inlets of Chichester Harbour with Bosham itself on the east and Chidham, opposite, on the west — the road down to the village skirts the water and gives delightful views. The church has a white-painted wooden porch which is unusual, and there's a thatched cottage called Crooked Chimney, for the best possible reason, as you'll know when you see it.

But Chidham is known for wheat. A Mr. Woods was walking out one day when he saw, growing wild in a bank, a type of wheat with an outsized ear. He took it home and planted it, and thence came a new prolific strain of the cereal which has ever since been known as Chidham wheat.   [30]

CHILGROVE

The lane descending from Heathbarn Down to West Dean is an ancient one, and you can verify this by counting the different kinds of trees in the hedge alongside it. Historical botanists have devised a pretty reliable rule of thumb for estimating the age of hedgerows. Count the number of species in a thirty-yard stretch, including trees and shrubs, but not brambles and nettles — each one represents about a hundred years. This hedge at Chilgrove had ten species when we last counted, indicating that it's been a boundary for at least a thousand years.

Farmers have worked the land here for much longer than this: a Roman villa was recently excavated alongside the lane, while another was found at Brick Kiln Farm, down by the B2141. Literally hundreds of amateur and professional archaeologists have been involved in the Chilgrove Valley Landscape Project, which is investigating Roman farming in relation to the military base at Chichester.   [17]

CHITHURST

'The church', says the Victoria County History, 'stands on a mound, probably artificial'. Arthur Mee says that the mound was originally a Saxon temple, but doesn't tell us how he knows. In any case, it dates from the eleventh century, in the period of the Saxo-Norman overlap (see *Introduction*). It may indeed be the very church mentioned in Domesday, and it looks as if, in its incredibly remote situation, very little had happened to it since. It's well perched up on its mound, and there's quite a drop on the south side down to the river. It has a number of very early tombstones, some almost buried under centuries of fallen leaves. Some of them may well be almost as old as the church.

Stop at the church gate and you'll see a fine topiary hedge beyond the entrance to the old manor house, now called Chithurst Abbey, although it never was a monastery. You can get closer, along the signposted public footpath; the day we went, there was a delightful gipsy caravan just round the corner, but we can't guarantee its permanence!   [8]

CLAPHAM

An entry in the church visitors' book reads: 'A very nice smelly place'. But it has other points of interest than the aroma, including a sharply 'weeping' chancel (see *Introduction*). Many generations of the Shelley family are buried here. There is a Tudor brass to a Shelley who died in 1526; he kneels in ruff and armour on the left, his son behind him, while his wife and daughter kneel facing him. A tomb recess in the chancel is of a later Shelley, Sir William (died 1548), his wife Alice, and fourteen children, neatly made up of seven of each sex. By the eighteenth century we have several monuments, including that of Wilhelmina Shelley, who died age 23, 'The Pride of her own Sex, the Admiration of ours'.

An attractive little toll cottage stands at the start of the road to Patching.
[19]

CLAYTON

For a small village Clayton has several attractions. Note the absurdly ornate Victorian embellishment at the entrance to the railway tunnel — castellated portals with arrowslits and battlemented turrets. The cottage which sits between the turrets is more recent and the occupants are subjected to continual subterranean rumblings.

The Jack and Jill windmills, on the hill above the village, can be seen from miles away. Jack is the black one, a brick tower mill built on the site in 1896. Jill (the white one) is a post mill and was hauled over the downs by teams of oxen from its original home at Patcham, Brighton.

Just along Underhill Lane, the church is a humble one but much-visited on account of its fine medieval wall-paintings, depicting scenes such as the Last Judgement, Christ in Glory and the Fall of Satan. In the churchyard is the grave of Sir Norman Hartnell, the Queen's dress designer for many years. **[20]**

CLIMPING

All that's left of the smock windmill is a two-storey fragment above the base, death-watch beetle having destroyed the timbers. The Post Office Pension Fund are its somewhat unlikely owners, but they've preserved it carefully.

The 'Crusader's chest' in the church dates from the thirteenth century, but was not used like a cabin trunk, to pack changes of chain-mail for bold knights fighting to recover the Holy Land! Observation shows there is a small slot in the top as if it were a money box — which is in fact just what it is. During King John's reign, Pope Innocent III ordered boxes or chests to be placed in all parish churches to receive donations by parishioners towards the cost of the Fifth Crusade. They were made thus large to make them difficult to steal by night. The modern paintings in the transept are not, as the label says, frescoes, but paintings on wood or canvas. Our picture shows the intricate two-layered Norman carving around the west door and window of the tower, which is very rare. [26]

COATES

'The Sussex weed' was the derogatory name given to the majestic oak in days gone by. The enchanting toy-like church shows how timber was used, with six great oak tie-beams to hold the roof, and a church door made of a double thickness of solid oak planking, set vertically on the outside, horizontally inside, and all held together by heavy iron strapping. It's 400 years old and was made to last — as it has.

Also in this tiny village less than two miles from Fittleworth is a fine barn and a 'castle' built in Gothic style in the early 19th century, but castellated and decked out as if it had time-warped from the Wars of the Roses. [9]

COCKING

Not even the exhaustive 'Dictionary of the Sussex Dialect' by the Rev. Parish (see *Selmeston*) gives 'Foxes-brewings'. But M. A. Lower's 'History' tells us that from the beechwoods on the Downs "there rises in unsettled weather a mist which rolls among the trees like the smoke out of a chimney. This exhalation is called 'Foxes-brewings', whatever that may mean, and if it tends westward towards Cocking rain follows speedily. Hence the local proverb:-

> *When Foxes-brewings go to Cocking,*
> *Foxes-brewings come back dropping. "*

We admit that we didn't wait to verify the maxim, but we did find the church, down a side lane, whch contains a wall-painting of c.1300 in the south aisle. In the chancel are several unusual monuments, including a seventeenth century plaque headed by a rosette of bones, a skull and similar gruesome symbols.

The guide-book is not sold in the church but in the local post office, shut at weekends at the times when most visitors will want to buy it.   [17]

COLDWALTHAM

Originally just 'Waltham', the prefix was added in the fourteenth century, because of its bleak situation. But did Frederick Harrison have to rub it in so hard in his 'Notes on Sussex Churches' by indexing it under 'Waltham (Cold)'? Anyway, just east of the village is a nature reserve area maintained by the Sussex Trust for Nature Conservation. It's readily identified by the butterfly plaque on a post in a field.

The church, originally Norman, founded a village school in 1750, which was able to celebrate its centenary in the same building. Opposite the church is a priest house (not used as such now) reputed to date from c.1220.   [9]

COLEMANS HATCH

The name goes back to Edmund and Richard Coleman in 1279, and 'hatch' signified a gate. The hamlet is on the edge of Ashdown Forest, with its splendid open views, and was one of seven original gates, or 'hatches', to the forest: Chuck Hatch is a mile or so to the east, Plaw Hatch south-west of Forest Row, and so on. The Hatch Inn is the centre of a little cluster of attractive houses.

The church dates from 1913; its interior is spacious and there are good copies of a couple of Italian Renaissance paintings.   [5]

COLGATE

A dragon, so 'tis said, used to lurk in St. Leonard's Forest, until Leonard himself (a French sixth century anchorite) killed it. As reward, it was granted to him that lilies of the valley would spring up wherever a drop of his blood had stained the earth. Colgate is in the middle of the Forest, and the beacon is the highest point in this part of Sussex. [4]

COLWORTH

A little straggle of houses off the A259 north-west of Bognor Regis, almost bisected by the line of the old Chichester-Arundel canal. With the aid of the ordnance map you can trace its line alongside the public footpath which starts beside Merston church and goes east through Lidsey and into Yapton. [18]

COMPTON

East of the church rises Telegraph Hill, named for the semaphore station which once stood on its summit. It was one of a series of prominently-sited stations used for relaying messages from Portsmouth Dockyard to the Admiralty in London, and energetic ramblers may still find traces of it.

A public bridleway leads near the summit down to Bevis's Thumb, a long barrow beside the lane to East Marden. Bevis was a legendary giant hailing from Southampton who often crossed to the Isle of Wight by wading. He was a warder at Arundel Castle, where he would eat a whole ox every week. [29]

CONEYHURST

Pennsylvania is a long way from Sussex, but its founder, William Penn, lived in the county after returning from America; he would walk from his home (see *Warminghurst*) to 'The Blue Idol' here to speak at Quaker meetings. The building, just outside the hamlet, down a side road but well signposted, offers overnight accommodation but is principally a Friends' Meeting House. The strange name has been explained in many ways; the most plausible is that it was once painted blue and was not in regular use — hence 'idle'. So it was a blue, idle meeting-house. Most books on Sussex place names discreetly omit it. [10]

COOLHAM

'Saddlers' is a tiny cottage right by the roadside of the B2139 road, just north of the village centre. It has only one door and one bay window facing the road. Could it have been a toll cottage, or was it perhaps correctly named as the workshop for the village saddle-maker? Perhaps the same man did both jobs.

[10]

COOMBES

A farmyard may not be the ideal approach to a little church, but here it helps to emphasise the country character. The churchyard has the only tapsel gate we found in West Sussex (see *Friston*). The west end of the church is almost dug into the steep hillside, and from the exterior it's clear that the nave was at some date widened on both north and south sides, by about a foot or so. Inside are some of the county's best wall paintings, including (on the chancel arch) a medieval Atlas figure, grimacing with the effort of holding up the world. Incredible that it's not much more than a mile off the busy A27. [20]

COPTHORNE

Like *Crawley Down*, if not on the same scale, Copthorne was once a centre for prize-fighting and in 1810 there was a celebrated bout on the common between the champion, Tom Cribb, and an American ex-slave, Tom Molyneux. Blood was spilt at other times, too, the common being renowned for attracting lawless characters. Tradition says that there was once a horn which hung here, so that a traveller could summon help if waylaid by footpads. [5]

COWFOLD

The impressive spire you see through the trees belongs to the strict and enclosed hermit order, the Carthusians. St. Hugh's monastery — the largest in England — was built in the 1880s to accommodate up to 200 religious fleeing persecution on the continent. In the event a new tolerance ensued, and today about a dozen monks and a few lay brothers occupy an echoing and austerely grand building, emerging only once a week for a quiet walk through the surrounding countryside.

Unhappily, you are even less likely to see the famed brass to Prior Nelond, which has lain for centuries in the middle of the nave of the parish church. It is hidden and protected under a locked carpet, and this is nothing new: sixty years ago, Harrison tells us, it was 'effectively protected by a padlocked covering'. It's generally accounted the largest brass in the whole of England, a magnificent specimen over ten feet in length and in good preservation. [11]

CRAWLEY DOWN

It's hard to imagine that the village green at Crawley Down — a modern, respectable dormitory for Gatwick Airport and Crawley — once resounded to the howls of a mob braying for blood. In Regency times it was a famed centre for prize-fighting. They were brutal occasions, continuing until one of the combatants was knocked senseless or failed to 'come up to scratch' — a mark in the middle of the ring. The Prince of Wales enjoyed the entertainment here, while another visitor was the poet John Keats. He was brought to one of the fights to take his mind off his brother's death. Literary references conjure up the image of a long procession of twinkling lights as the fashionable carriages made their way to the scene from London and Brighton. [5]

CROSS BUSH

Almost opposite the Lyminster road from the A27, a clock tower a bit like an ornamental birdcage looks out over a high wall. It belongs to a convent of Poor Clares, an enclosed order of nuns. [18]

CROSS IN HAND

Naughty goings-on in the park led to the moving of Cross in Hand mill which, like many another, has had several homes and has answered to several names. It was built at Framfield in 1806, but it's said that Squire Huth objected to its overlooking his park at Possingworth where unseemly happenings were rumoured to occur. Having been Mount Ephraim mill and then Kenward's mill, it was moved to Cross in Hand as the New mill. In 1969, while grinding corn, one of the sweeps broke away and badly damaged another — and that was the end of its working life. [13]

CROWBOROUGH

Once a centre of the Sussex iron industry, Crowborough is now mainly residential, and, indeed, is nearly a town. Steel Cross is on the north-eastern outskirts, but has nothing to do with the metal. It comes from Richard le Stile who held land here in 1296. The beacon at over 800 feet is the highest point for miles, and extensive views can still be enjoyed. It was a favourite haunt of smugglers, one of whom is believed still to ride with a lantern searching for his loot. [6]

CROWHURST

Many are the Sussex churchyards boasting a venerable yew, but the one at Crowhurst is clearly very ancient indeed. Now supported in its old age, and cracked so that a grown man could stand inside the bole, it has a girth of well over 40 feet. The guide book claims that it's 'at least a thousand years old'. Relative newcomers are the nearby remains of the old manor house, thought to date from the twelfth century. [24]

CROWLINK

The cellars of Crowlink House were reputedly the store for 'Genuine Crowlink' — a smuggled gin which fetched a high price in the nineteenth century. The last serious skirmish near here was at Flagstaff Point in 1782, when two smugglers and one exciseman were killed.

Leave your car just beyond Friston church and you can walk into the hamlet of Crowlink — once a working estate but now with most of its buildings converted into private homes. A circular journey along well marked footpaths makes an excellent outing on a fine day. [28]

CUCKFIELD

Tenpence in a little box near the church door will light up the vault for you. The roof itself is fifteenth century, but C. E. Kempe did the painting in 1886. When the roof was built, the wall-posts in several cases came right over the clearstorey windows, which were blocked up. They were uncovered as recently as 1925; notice how on the north side of the nave the upper windows are centred between the arches, but not on the south.

Two items of interest: a picturesque row of three cottages whose front doors open directly onto the churchyard and, a little way up the hill, the small but well-stocked and well-run village museum. [11]

DALLINGTON

'Mad Jack' Fuller erected the so-called Sugar Loaf in a field north of the B2906 at Woods Corner, allegedly to win a bet (see illustration under *Brightling*). The story goes that one night, during a rowdy party, he wagered that the spire of Dallington church (now, incidentally, one of the three remaining stone spires in Sussex) could be seen from his house. Discovering that this wasn't so, he promptly had a look-alike put up. Fortunately no evidence has ever been put forward to ruin this splendid tale.

The church is, in fact, at a lower level down a minor road. Around it clusters a delightful group of houses, one of them timber-framed and worth a good analytical look. Inside, an undated board by the door on the south wall records that 'The Incorporated Society for Building &c Churches granted £100 towards rebuilding this church, upon condition that 331 seats, numbered 1 to 40, be reserved for the use of the poorer inhabitants of this parish'. The original numbers can still be seen, but a few of the pews are missing. Let us hope that this signifies a growing prosperity in the village!

[14]

DANEHILL

The Victorian church may well claim to have the most imposing situation of any Sussex church. It stands overlooking the little village crossroads, near which (down the Freshfield road) stands the house formerly occupied by the village blacksmith. He made himself a front gate including the words 'Etherton – Smith', with a design of butterflies on either side. It's a lovely example of unpretentious craftsmanship. [12]

DELL QUAY

Incredibly, this, recently described as the tiniest port in Britain, once ranked as the ninth in the whole country. It was in Roman times the port for Chichester, and most likely all the building materials for the Fishbourne palace passed by here. At low tide you get a fine view across the Chichester Channel, and one of the Cathedral from the approach road.

The mill here was insured two hundred years ago for two hundred pounds. It was a working mill until about 1870, and the tower part was dismantled, leaving simply the roundhouse. This has been ingeniously built into a private house, where it stands for anyone to see, and yet is not readily recognisable. [30]

DENTON

We don't know if there is, or ever was, a font made out of a basket, but the font in this church is covered with an interlacing basketwork type of design, with rows of small pellets above and below. It is almost unique in that its only counterpart is at St. Anne's, Lewes. This type of design was a trade-mark, as it were, of the Comacini, a group of twelfth century sculptors of French-Italian provenance, whose name probably comes from the Italian lake town of Como. They often travelled to England and were commissioned to do work here. From the west end of the churchyard may be seen the remains of a thirteenth century priest house, and there is a small but clear mass dial on the south-west buttress. [27]

DIAL POST

The gaunt fragment of a medieval castle stands on a knoll about a mile north of the hamlet of Dial Post, beside the A24 road. It's all that is left of old Knepp Castle, a fortress of importance in the twelfth and thirteenth centuries — King John visited it several times. It was built soon after the Norman Conquest by the lords of Bramber and belonged for many years to the family of William de Braose, lord of many estates in Sussex. [10]

DIDLING

The light switch by the door is so much a part of our lives that one is surprised to find a church without one. St. Andrew, Didling, along a narrow lane where it's better to walk (there's nowhere to turn your car) is still lit by candles and a single oil lamp. Apart from a nave chandelier and a chancel wall-bracket, the only light comes from a single candle in a holder at the end of each pew. The pews themselves deserve a glance: they are nearly all over 400 years old. [8]

DITCHLING

In a village full of antiquity, Wings Place opposite the church must be accounted the most spectacular house. Tradition has it that it was one of those given by Henry VIII to Anne of Cleves, and it was at one time known as The Royal Palace. It is certainly 500 years old; but in 1894 it was put up for auction, when the particulars described it as 'an Ancient Mansion (now let in tenements) of great Historical and Antiquarian Interest, known as 'Wings Place', said to have been built by King Alfred the Great, and believed to be described in Doomsday Book, but the Vendors do not guarantee the accuracy of these statements . . .' And all before the Trade Descriptions Act!

Between it and the crossroads is a house faced with mathematical tiles, red and black. It's far from clear how these tiles got their name, but the idea is that they are shaped so that when fitted together and hung vertically they look like bricks. They are a peculiarly local product, and the best range of them can be seen at Lewes.

The road up to Ditchling Beacon is narrow and winding, but must not be missed. The National Trust, who own the land around, have recently constructed a new car-park, ingeniously concealed. The nearby tumuli, dewpond and other interesting features are easily reached.

Anne of Cleves may or may not have actually lived here, but among more recent residents have been the artists Frank Brangwyn and Eric Gill. Numerous personalities of stage and television still do enhance the village — though we shall preserve their peace by leaving them unnamed.   [20]

DONNINGTON

Part of the Chichester-Arundel Canal (see *Birdham, Hunston*), runs through open fields here. Equally open is the church, approached by a rough lane and fire-damaged in 1939. The tower remains, very un-Sussex with its battlements, with, high up, flint crosses on Calvary steps, on two faces.

A nineteenth century writer reported that Donnington was at one time the worst reputed village in the county for smuggling; the church was store for many cargoes of rum and tobacco. Happily, a succession of good clergymen and the construction of a school worked such wonders that 'Donnington became the third best conducted parish in England'. One wonders why specifically third. [25]

DOWN STREET

At the bottom of the lane from Splaynes Green is a small stream which is the begining of the River Ouse. Nearby, Daleham (now spelt Dale Hamme) is an early Tudor house with moulded beams and uprights a-twist, as Sussex folk would say. Like many other old houses, its 'underground passage' was only an arched drain. [5]

DUNCTON

At the top of Duncton Hill on the A285 is a lime quarry. Lime kilns have stood in this area for well over a hundred years, and one from the mid-nineteenth century may still be found in eerie isolation along a bridle path leading off the road near the foot of the hill. It's really a three-in-one, as you'll see. Elsewhere in the village is a disused watermill with an iron overshot wheel, some of the wooden machinery and three pairs of stones. The Southern Water Authority leases the pond for fish farming, so a commercial use continues.

Invisible, but not inaudible, is the bell of the Victorian parish church further north. Harrison's Handbook to Sussex Churches notes that the bell is Dutch and, bearing the date 1369, is the oldest dated bell in Sussex. [9]

DURFORD ABBEY

Durford Abbey (or Dureford, but not nowadays Durfold, though it was so named at the Dissolution) is west of Rogate, as near as one can get to, without crossing, the county boundary into Hampshire. It stands off a layby. Apart from a few pieces of carved stone used in constructing a garden wall, there is nothing left. But in its day Durford was a large abbey of Premonstratensian Canons, founded in 1160 and at the Dissolution worth the then large sum of £100 a year. [29]

EARNLEY

The last full working windmill in Sussex, it's believed, is here; the business closed as recently as 1946. An octagonal, black-tarred, weather boarded smock mill of three floors, it apparently dates from the eighteenth century. It's claimed that two of the old millstones now form part of the crazy paving laid down in a garden nearby.

The thirteenth century church lies about a mile south of the mill. The welded iron altar cross and candlesticks were made from tractor parts by Mr. John Rusbridge of Earnley Manor; Mrs. Yvonne Rusbridge designed the nave tile patterns. [25]

EARTHAM

Stephenson's 'Rocket' was the first railway engine — it also produced the first railway fatality. William Huskisson, MP for Chichester, was the victim, killed in 1830. He lived at Bowden House, across Eartham churchyard wall.

In the far corner of the churchyard is a small round garden pavilion now roofed over and provided with a chimney pot, most unexpectedly, and a weather vane: could it once have been a dovecote?

Over the churchyard wall, in the grounds of the adjacent preparatory school, you can see an eighteenth-century orangery, with bow front. Unhappily, it is now roofless and devoid of the glass of its windows. It was built of brick with rock-work bands all the way up and along the fascia. It is very pretty but very un-English; the inspiration must have come from France. [17/18]

EASEBOURNE

A strange-looking structure across the road from the priory looks like a gateless lych-gate. It was once a cattle grid for horse traffic, and the old inscription remains. Impatient motorists still use it when Cowdray polo traffic causes congestion.

The buildings of the former priory of Augustinian canonesses are now incorporated into a private house, but from the public footpath (without invading the privacy of the occupants) you get a glimpse of the former cloister walls.

The nuns had a reputation for profligacy: in 1440 the then prioress was suspended for excessive expenditure and fineries! [8]

EAST CHILTINGTON

Inflation isn't all that new — it's been going on for centuries, as the church here shows. The sign to the 'Jolly Sportsman' leads you over an old Roman road, marked on the Ordnance map but not clearly visible, to the church as well as the pub. The vestry beneath the tower has charity boards on the walls, recording perpetual gifts of sums like £4 6s. 8d. (£4.33p) which in the seventeenth century was quite a fair sum. Trustees still administer the charities even today.

[21]

EAST DEAN (East Sussex)

The row of flint buildings which includes the Tiger Inn was once the barracks for the local militia. Nearby Birling Gap was a (literal) haven for smugglers, who evidently gave the excisemen a hard time of it. Up on the cliffs is Belle Tout lighthouse, in a prominent position but unfortunately fogbound (and hence useless) for about six months in every year. The light had to be moved along to Beachy Head, so that the building is now a private residence.

[28]

EAST DEAN (West Sussex)

Flint is a useful and durable building material (see *Introduction*). Many of the older buildings here are flint with brick features; a charming contrast. But one group, opposite the 'Star and Garter' pub, has quoins (the angles formed by two adjoining walls) of knapped flint, wonderfully accurately made, the sharp corners of each stone forming a crisp corner to each wall.

Our illustration shows an old gravestone in the wall of the south transept, on the eastern exterior of the church.   [17]

EASTERGATE

Next to the parish church is Manor Farm — indeed, you almost go through the farmyard to reach the church. The farm granary must be one of the most magnificent buildings in the county; it's late Elizabethan or early Stuart in date, although of necessity it has received some restoration. It stands on contemporary staddlestones (mushroom-shaped stands both helping air to circulate underneath and posing an insoluble problem for rats trying to get inside), and the walls are of bold half-timbered brick. If you can drag yourself away, inside the church is a rarity — a pair of priests' stalls, one on either side of the chancel entry, each with twin pillars of turned wood supporting a wooden canopy or tester in a severely classical style which looks oddly out-of-place in the much earlier surroundings. One of the comparatively few pieces of medieval glass is the coat of arms in one of the south windows: it dates from about 1360. [18]

EAST GULDEFORD

If anyone thinks that Romney Marsh is entirely in Kent, here is the place to disprove it, even if only just. In the fifteenth century much of the flat marshland was salt, and quite a local industry was pursued. About 1498 it was 'inned' (the Sussex word for enclosed from the sea) and a ferry was set up for foot passengers which continued to give a useful service for four centuries.

Almost immediately work started on building the church which was consecrated in 1505. It's one of only three churches in Sussex built of Tudor brick (the others are at *Egdean* and *Twineham*). The bricks are worth a look: they're smaller and flatter than modern bricks, and are laid in 'English bond' — courses of headers and stretchers alternating. [16]

EASTHAMPNETT

Like most counties, Sussex has its traditional design of cart. There is an authentic one, beautifully preserved, in the forecourt of the Winterton Arms pub, very picturesque in this tiny hamlet of scarcely more than a dozen homes. Earl Winterton was a prominent local landowner and an M.P.   [17]

EAST HOATHLY

A green plaque on a corner terrace house near the sharp bend at the centre of the village marks the place where Thomas Turner lived. Turner (1729-1789) was the local Samuel Pepys, a schoolmaster and general dealer best known for the diary he kept — an edition of which has been recently published. He writes frequently of the running battle of wills with his difficult wife (until she dies and becomes, in retrospect, an angel), and of his lamentable fondness for drink:

> *Oh! a melancholy thing it is to deprive oneself of reason, and even to render ourselves beasts! ... We drank health and success to his Majesty and the Royal Family, the King of Prussia, Prince Ferdinand of Brunswick, Lord Anson, his Grace the Duke of Newcastle and his Duchess, Lord Abergavenny, Admiral Boscawen, Mr. Pelham of Stanmore, the Earl of Ancram, Lord Gage, Marshall Keith, and several more loyall healths. About ten I deserted, and come safe home; but to my shame do I mention it, very much in liquor.*

In the church, admire the east wall of the chancel, lavishly decorated in mosaic in a pre-Raphaelitish style — tasteful blues, reddish browns, yellows and patches of gilt. This was provided by the children of the Reverend Frederick Borradaile and his wife Demetria towards the end of the last century. Among the features are the archangels Gabriel, Michael, Uriel and Raphael, with a lamb as the centrepiece.   [22]

EAST LAVINGTON (see Woolavington)

EAST MARDEN

A delightful thatched well-head (illustrated under *Mardens*) occupies the centre of the tiny village green. The church peers down at it from a slight elevation, and there are a few cottages, most over 200 years old. For the late twentieth century, unbelievably remote and peaceful. We love it.   [29]

EAST PRESTON

The hanging of a labourer involved in the so-called Swing Riots led to the building of the old East Preston school in Sea Road — now the offices of estate agents King & Chasemore. Rural unrest spread through Sussex in the autumn of 1830, farmers receiving threatening letters from the notorious (and almost certainly non-existent) Captain Swing. Workers, incensed by the introduction of threshing machines, demanded higher wages. There were several outbreaks of arson in the area and Edmund Bushby of East Preston, a 26-year-old labourer, was publicly hanged outside the gate of Horsham gaol on New Year's Day 1831 for setting fire to a hayrick at Homestead Farm. His boss, George Olliver, picked up a reward of £500 for information leading to the arrest and conviction. Olliver used the cash to endow a Sunday school for teaching the poor children of East Preston and Kingston to read, and to give them a grounding in the Protestant religion. It was built in 1840.

'As the hour of twelve drew nigh', we learn from a contemporary account of the hanging, 'numbers of labouring men from the surrounding parishes flocked into the town, and at noon from 800 to a thousand persons had assembled in front of the gaol . . . Bushby ascended the scaffold with a firm step . . . he briefly addressed the spectators, exhorting them to take warning by his end and pay a diligent regard to the Sabbath . . . the bolt was drawn and Bushby was speedily no more'.   [26]

EBERNOE

'An improbable enchanted place', says Ian Nairn — but on July 25 there takes place each year a Horn Fair of immemorial tradition. The main event is a cricket match in which the highest scoring batsman is awarded a pair of sheep's horns — plus, nowadays, the rest of the head which has been roasted as part of the festivities. The hamlet contains a diminutive Victorian chapel, a plain but rather grand eighteenth century house, and very little besides.   [9]

EDBURTON

Missionaries nearly 300 years ago had stout hearts indeed. The Society for the Propagation of the Gospel, founded in the late seventeenth century, sent its first missionary to America in 1702, in the Admiralty ship 'Centurion'. He was the Rev. George Keith, who on his return in 1705 became rector of Edburton. To commemorate the 250th anniversary of their work, in 1951 the S.P.G. gave the church a stained-glass replica of their common seal, which now adorns the east window in the south nave wall.

Here is one of only three lead fonts in Sussex, and here too is a good seventeenth century 'black-letter' bible, now kept in a glass case but originally chained to the reading desk now on the north side of the nave. The old chain is still on the desk, while under it are the old bell clappers, of impressive size and weight.   [20]

EGDEAN

The church (and there is very little else) is one of three in Sussex built of old seventeenth century brick. The south doorway shows a bit of the work, but it nearly all vanished in a so-called 'restoration' in the nineteenth century.[9]

ELSTED

The eleventh-century church owes its survival in a strange way, to a church a mile off. When the second, Victorian, church was built at *Treyford* St. Paul's, Elsted, was allowed to become derelict. Then Treyford church was demolished in 1951 and Elsted was sympathetically restored and brought back into use.

The Platts, a house in the village, has clear and interesting indications on its exterior how it has been extended and altered over the centuries. [8]

ERIDGE

On a drive around Eridge you'll see — on inns, lodges and cottages over several miles — a striking heraldic device: a bull with Tudor rose and portcullis and a large 'A' tied with tassels. This is the device of the Marquess of Abergavenny, who holds sway in Eridge Park. A large country house built in 1938 replaces the old castle which was situated nearer to the Frant end of the park.

The great estates of Sussex are now largely broken up, but here at Eridge you can witness a modern throwback to feudal times in the parish church, where the Abergavenny pews are segregated by a gate across the aisle and have their own entrance at the west end. It can't be denied, however, that the family has earned this mark of respect. The church, which was built in 1851 at the cost of the then Earl of Abergavenny, was beautifully restored in 1950 thanks to the generosity of the fourth Marquess and Marchioness. The interior contains the craftsmanship of workmen from throughout the county. [6]

ETCHINGHAM

The great horses no longer pull ploughs across the Sussex landscape, but John and Brenda Lavis at Haremere Hall are convinced that there will again be a place for them on the big estates. Your modern show horse is a long-legged, narrow-chested fellow and crossing with hunters had made him uncertain of temperament. Now the Lavises are breeding back the old-fashioned kind of horse, crossing modern shires with more humble down-to-earth creatures. One of their foals, Lord Napoleon, has been adopted by BBC Radio Sussex: with his stable companions, he is on show daily to the public.

In the parish church (once moated: parts of it can still be traced) is the oldest dated brass in Sussex, depicting the fourteenth-century William de Echyngham. There is also the largest series of misericords in Sussex apart from those in Chichester cathedral. Misericords are small 'comfort' ledges under tip-up stalls, designed to afford a slight rest for monks or others who could not stand during the long medieval services. They were often carved with leaves, columns or decorations; look for one depicting a fox preaching to geese. [15]

EWHURST GREEN

An Edwardian tragedy is commemorated in a 'corona', or chandelier, and in a window of the church. William Jacobson, baptised on September 26, 1899, drowned in a pond in his father's garden at Lordine Farm on March 16, 1905. In the window he is shown sitting on Christ's knee, and various texts testify to his parents' efforts to understand their loss: 'My thoughts are not your thoughts, neither are your ways my ways saith the Lord.' After his death his parents emptied his money box and put the cash towards a corona for the oil lamps then used in the church. It hangs in the nave and is now electrified.[15]

EXCEAT

Raiders from France in the middle ages brought death to this village near the mouth of the Cuckmere. (Many people pronounce it 'Exy-at', but old maps spell it 'Excete' or a variation of it, so perhaps 'Ex-seet' is authentic. Analogies with schoolday 'exeats' are fallacious, not to say misleading!). Once it was quite an important fishing village, but repeated incursions by French raiding-parties caused the population to decline to extinction by the early sixteenth century. It was excavated before World War 2, and the Sussex Archaeological Society erected a tablet on the site of the old church. Nearby is the East Sussex County Council information centre, and the Forestry Commission has set out a number of enjoyable woodland walks.

Also here is The Living World, a fascinating museum of live insects, fish and small creatures of all kinds. [28]

FAIRLIGHT

At Fairlight country park (just beyond the car park) is a memorial to the man known as Grey Owl. He claimed to have been born in Mexico of a Scottish father and a North American Indian mother, and he came to England in the thirties to give highly popular lecture tours about his (then novel) conservation work in Canada. He gave a command performance at Buckingham Palace, during which the young Princess Elizabeth became greatly excited.

In fact he was a former Hastings grammar school boy, Archie Belaney, who had immersed himself in Indian culture from boyhood and who had left England for Canada in his teens to become an expert trapper. He lived a wandering and tempestuous life until, inspired by his Indian wife Anahareo, he discovered the cause of wildlife preservation, wrote several books on the subject and preached the message of 'natural brotherhood between man and animals'. [24]

FAIRWARP

Messages go all over the world from the hilltop at Duddleswell, for here is the Foreign Office's diplomatic wireless service station, by means of which London maintains contact with its embassies and legations all over the world. You can't miss the scores of radio masts inside their fenced enclosure. [12]

FALMER

Geese and ducks still inhabit the village pond, better for its isolation since the A27 arrived. Beside it stands a (handleless) village pump, bearing no maker's name — just a lion's head and the proud legend 'Made in England'. Hard by, a row of four flint-and-brick cottages has its own story. The roof of the group must at some time have been raised. New windows were inserted as dormers but the brick outline of the old windows is still clear; their irregularity makes it hard to visualise how the little group must originally have looked. [21]

FAYGATE

The Holmbush Inn has a survival from the early days of motoring. On its front wall is a circular yellow-and-black enamelled sign of the type which the AA used to put up everywhere as village signs: they were removed during World War 2 to avoid giving away locations to possible enemy parachutists. The Faygate one is the first we remember seeing in the whole county. [4]

FELPHAM

William Blake, poet, painter and mystic, and one of England's most original geniuses, lived here from 1800-03. His house is still called 'Blake's Cottage', and is in Blake Road, near Hayley's Corner. Hayley was a poet and the intimate of many of the greats of his day, and invited Blake to live near him so that the two could collaborate on illustrations for a book, which Hayley was writing. Blake always afterwards thought of Felpham as Heaven.

For those interested in more industrial matters, a few yards down Upper Bognor Road from the holiday camp is a nineteenth century sluice gate with its wooden 'shutters' and cable drums still in working order.   [26]

FERNHURST

Hidden among the woods which once surrounded Verdley Castle, of which only a few bits of wall remain, is the plant protection division of I.C.I., which has been beautifully landscaped. To drive along the surrounding roads must excite admiration in almost any heart, but if that leaves you unmoved, try the village green, which must be among the most delightful anywhere.

Verdley Castle was a ruin by the early nineteenth century; by mid-century most of its stones had been taken away and broken up for use in the new macadam roads.

A large iron foundry was casting Government cannon here as late as 1770 — it was the last ironworks in West Sussex.   [1]

FERRING

Fixed to the south pillar of the chancel arch in St. Andrew's church is an hourglass stand. With the Reformation, preaching and the pulpit were emphasised at the expense of ceremony and the altar — a trend that was to be put into reverse in later Victorian times. It's tempting to imagine the congregation willing the sand to sift swiftly through the neck of the glass.[26]

FINDON

On either side of the A24 and the village are hills of great interest to archaeologists. Eastward lies the vast hilltop fort of Cissbury, covering some 60 acres and holding over 200 flint mines, visible as crater-like depressions in the turf. To the west, Church Hill towers above the fascinating old church. Here were more flint mines dating back (if the radio-carbon analysis of an antler pick found here is correct) to before 4,000 B.C.   [19]

FIRLE

The first entry in this book (*Adversane*) mentions the two main Roman roads in Sussex. The Rabbit Walk at Firle is an example of a minor one.

Park your car at the top of Firle Beacon. The track leads eastwards along the top, and the Rabbit Walk can't be seen from there. Follow the fence line below the crest and you'll come across a narrow terrace eight feet wide, and with a clear drainage channel on the inner side.

The Roman method was to build an embankment, or *agger*, with ditches to either side. The Rabbit Walk leads obliquely down the hillside before turning north towards Firle Park. This is part of a local road which connected the settlement at Seaford with a further road complex at Ripe in the valley below.

Officially the village is West Firle — but there is no East or other Firle. On the outskirts stands Firle Place, home of the Gage family for centuries. It's regularly open during the summer months and contains a superb collection of furniture and works of art.

The whole village is pervaded by the Gage aura; the village reading-room was given by public subscription in 1913 in honour of the then Viscount, and it has the initial 'G' and a coronet over the door. One of the Gages, Thomas, was a botanist, and he's credited with introducing (and giving his name to) the greengage in England. He planted the fruit here.

There are two mass dials (see *Introduction*) on the church wall, but both are on the right-hand jamb of the *North* door, where no sun would reach. So the doorway must have been dismantled at some date and re-erected.   [21]

FISHBOURNE

So celebrated is the Roman palace at Fishbourne that it's startling to reflect that its existence was unknown until 1960, when a workman unearthed some ancient-looking rubble while cutting a water-main trench.

Villas were scattered about the West Sussex landscape in Roman times, but this was something very different — a large and sumptuous building which is thought to have been the residence of King Cogidubnus, a British leader who threw in his lot with the invaders.

In those times the sea infiltrated further north than it does now, giving the Romans deep-water anchorage in Fishbourne harbour. This, then, was a prosperous area, and the palace itself was enlarged and improved over the centuries.

The evidence for all this, and for the fire which destroyed the building in the late third century, is presented in the best modern fashion — walls, mosaics, pots, statues, all clearly set out and explained in the museum adjoining the actual site remains.   [17]

FITTLEWORTH

Coaching inns are usually associated with main roads and large villages or towns. But at quiet Fittleworth is the Swan Inn, carrying a plaque saying that it's listed as of architectural and historic interest. Originally two fourteenth-century cottages, it once had a gantry sign straddling the road. Opposite is a fine barn, and up the road a Georgian house with a varied selection of door-cases.

In Brinkwells, off a minor road outside the village, Edward Elgar lived during the summers from 1917 to 1921: here he composed his Cello Concerto and his best-known chamber music including the String Quartet. [9]

FLETCHING

In the church lie the mortal remains of Edward Gibbon, author of the most famous history book ever written — 'The Decline and Fall of the Roman Empire'. In the north aisle of the church is a small brass to Peter Dynot, one of Jack Cade's followers (see *Cade Street*).

In the south transept is another great tomb telling an intriguing story. The inscription on Richard Leche's monument says that he 'gave all his landes in this county of Sussex unto Charitye his wife . . . and made her sole Executrix of his laste Will — in regard whereof, and for a perpetuall memorye of divers other charitable deedes that hee willed should be done; shee of her owne accorde caused this monument to be made, and herself living to be pictured lyinge by him as you see'. [12]

FOLKINGTON

The locals call it 'Fowenton'. Almost every house has charm — for instance, the one on the left, just off the main road, with a carved wooden gable dated 1880.

The church still retains half-a-dozen box pews, one on two levels and two with a central rail for hymn-books. One monument on the north wall is to Viscount Monckton, who lived at the Old Rectory, and who as Sir Walter Monckton was adviser to King Edward VIII during the Abdication.

Another nearby, is to Mrs. Violet Gordon Woodhouse (1871-1948), almost the first person in England to revive interest in music written for early keyboard instruments. She made a few tinkly records in the 1920s. The stone rightly says 'Born with a rare genius for music, her playing of the harpsichord and clavichord revealed a forgotten world of Beauty and Imagination, and the echoes of her music will sound for ever in the hearts of those that loved her'. [28]

FORD

The name nowadays generally means the Open Prison, but during the second world war it was an important airfield for fighter aircraft. Some of the old buildings, now used as barns and sheds, are visible from the Climping road or along Ford Lane.

The church is accessible only by walking across a field whose humps and bumps partially reveal the existence of foundations of a former moated mansion of the Bohun family. It is not in regular use, and we hear a rumour that it may be declared redundant. It will be a shame to lose it; Ian Nairn calls it one of the county's prettiest churches. Close by the only churchyard gate is a set of brick mounting steps, both inside and outside the wall: we illustrate them. Their purpose is obscure. They can't be a wall-stile, with the gate only a few feet away; and as mounting steps, they would be awkward, unless (as closer inspection reveals as a possibility) the wall was built after and 'through' the steps.   [18]

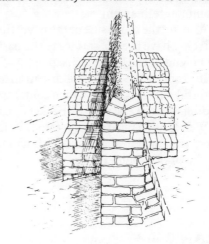

FOREST ROW

In the grounds of the health centre is a tree with suitably medical associations. The seed came from the oriental plane tree on the Greek island of Kos under which the founder of modern medicine, Hippocrates, was said to teach. The existing tree can't possibly be as old as that, but it's pleasant to believe that it may be a descendant. A local GP, Alan del Mar, was given some of the seeds by one of his patients. He germinated them, planted one sapling on the grave of his deceased basset hound, gave another to Wakehurst Place and put the third outside the health centre, where it's now about four feet high.

On the main A22 road to East Grinstead is a sign indicating the Forest Way, a fine track for walkers. Along it to the east are the remains of Brambletye House, the impressive ruin of the house built in 1631 for Sir Henry Compton. At the angles it had four-storey towers, one of which still stands at full height and wears its cap. Horace Smith wrote a now-forgotten novel in Victorian days entitled 'Brambletye House', set in the times when it was still lived in.   [5]

FRAMFIELD

Children playing games are not often seen in stained-glass windows in churches, but a modern window in Framfield church is one example. It was erected in the 1960s in memory of Arthur Haire, vicar of the parish for 22 years, who clearly believed in Christ's saying, 'Suffer little children to come unto me'. You can see children of various races picking flowers, playing with a hoop, and so on.

The church once had a rood-loft (see *Introduction*) reached by a stair and a double archway, so that it could be reached from either nave or chancel — an uncommon refinement.

Also, on the south side of the nave, there is an acutely angled squint which could only have been of service to the part of the congregation stationed at the very far end of the south transept.

In front of the north porch entrance to the churchyard is an unusually delightful village 'square' which contains several cottages in different styles of building. On the east side is 'Beckets', partly dating back to about 1400.

Well hidden until you get into the churchyard is an astonishing chimney turret, octagonal in shape and with windows high up in it. One wonders just how the smoke found its way out!   [13]

FRANT

Maps have given pleasure and education to people for centuries, but not until about 1700 were they thought of as guides.

None of the earlier maps such as John Speed's show any roads. But in the early eighteenth century a family named Budgen became surveyors and mapmakers, and by 1724 Richard Budgen had made a large-scale survey, including roads, of the whole of Sussex. He was born in Frant in 1680 and brought Shernfold Park, a house still shown on the Ordnance map at the south of the village. But the present house is Victorian, built after the earlier house had been owned by an army officer named John By who earned distinction in Canada and founded a town there which was then called Bytown but is now known as Ottawa.

A few years before Queen Victoria came to the throne Frant had a new church built in a strange style for remote Sussex. The pillars in the nave are of cast iron and support a canted ceiling. In 1892 were added a reading desk and pulpit of very Italianate solid alabaster.

The lych-gate is modern, and is a rarity in being hexagonal, for no very evident reason. Just by the church are the magnificent gates to Ely Grange, now the home of a big insurance company.   [6]

FRISTON

Distance in time lends enchantment even to vandalism: in the stone south porch of Friston church are crudely carved graffiti centuries old. The porch door is dedicated to the memory of Frank Bridge (1879-1941), the distinguished composer and first teacher of Benjamin Britten. A tablet on the wall depicts a music stave with the two notes F and B. Not far from his grave in the churchyard is a simple wooden cross with no name but a grim story in two words: 'washed ashore'. There are no names, either, on several headstones which mark the final resting places of merchant seamen lost during the last war. Each carries the inscription 'Known Unto God'. You enter the churchyard through what's become a rarity in Sussex — a tapsel gate pivoting on a central pillar.   [28]

FULKING

A copious spring flows beside, and indeed almost over, the village street. It's just below the Shepherd & Dog pub, and beside it is a wellhouse. On the side of the wellhouse is a text in Victorian tiles, one letter or a bit of decoration on each tile. It reads, 'He sendeth springs into the valleys which run among the hills. Oh that men would praise the Lord for His goodness'. It's a pity that the tilesetters put three of the 'S's upside-down, though the result is pleasantly rustic and 'unprofessional'.

Half a mile of so west of the village is Perching Manor Farm, with an eye-catching gateway surmounted by a dovecote. Almost opposite the farm entrance, near the summit of Edburton Hill, are the remains of a 'motte and bailey' fort — a small rectangular mound and ditch known as Castle Rings and probably constructed soon after the Norman invasion of 1066.   [20]

FUNTINGTON

A minor architectural puzzle is posed by a pair of cottages, Christmas Cottage and Yew Tree Cottage, which share identical roofs and a continuous moulded cornice under the eaves. But one of the pair is timber framed, the other all of brick. Clearly the roof must be a renewal, but what about the cornice?

One of the houses carries in its stonework an old insurance 'fire mark' with a picture of (presumably) Chichester cathedral. In days before municipal or county fire brigades and in the infancy of insurance, the insurance companies ran their own fire brigades. If you insured with one of them (which only the wealthy did), you were given a sign in the form of a small tablet to put up on the front of your house so that if you did suffer a fire, everyone knew which team of fire-fighters to call out.   [30]

GLYNDE

Hessian is, one would think, strictly as modern a wall-covering as you can get; but here is hessian, or something like it, used to cover the walls of a classical (non-Gothic) church. The building itself is hardly the most elegantly-proportioned one from the exterior; inside the classical motif is continued with carved woodwork, and deep octagonal coffering round the windows. It is next to Glynde Place and originally served as chapel for the house, which dates from about 1560, though the church is two centuries later. John Ellman, who first reared the Southdown sheep, is buried here.   [21]

GOODWOOD

The racecourse lies amid a setting which has rightly earned the sobriquet 'glorious'. It is overlooked by the Trundle, a massive Iron-Age hillfort to the west. Among the complicated ramparts and ditches you can trace the gates and structures of the fort and the site of the older causewayed camp. More recently the Trundle has seen a chapel of St. Roche (fifteenth century), a windmill (burnt out in 1773) and radio masts (definitely twentieth century). There is a local legend that the Golden Calf is buried somewhere in the huge mound!

Goodwood House, built by James Wyatt shortly before 1800 for the then Duke of Richmond, is still owned by and occupied by his descendants — it is regularly open to the public and its treasures include paintings by Canaletto, Turner, Stubbs and many more.

Before the advent of refrigerators, every big estate had to have an ice-house, carefully designed so that blocks of ice would remain to keep stores cold all through the summer. They were sited among trees to ward off the sun's warmth; the one at Goodwood is not far from the house, and its entrance is camouflaged to look like a garden pavilion. Close by it is the grave of Busaco, the fifth Duke's horse during the Peninsular War.   [17]

GRAFFHAM

A semi-detached chimney-stack must be rare, but the one on Stoberry Cottage looks like that, with its own separate sloping tiled roof. Nearby Rose Cottage has been altered and restored many times over the centuries, and is proud of its scars. If one may be forgiven the paradox, it's a unified jumble of great charm.

The church is over-restored, although the stubby columns (capitals only five feet above floor level) may raise an eyebrow. But the vestry door ought to raise two; first for the great age of the door itself, and second for the fifteenth century or earlier lock, which incredibly survives on the vestry side.   [9]

GRAVETYE

The grounds of Gravetye Manor were once a place of pilgrimage for horticulturists, because this was the home of William Robinson, 'the father of the English garden', who inveighed against formal bedding schemes and advocated a more naturalistic effect. The gardens have been partly restored and are open to the public twice a week.   [5]

GREATHAM

On the west side of the village, along the Coldwaltham road, and to the south, is a lovely timbered house called Quell with a thatched roof, recently renewed. The thatcher, well known in West Sussex for his craftsmanship, has decorated the roof ridge with his 'trade mark', a common practice. A pair of straw peacocks look as if they are about to peck the roof itself. The birds are modelled on a foundation shape like wire netting (see *Lancing*).   [9/10]

GROOMBRIDGE

From our point of view, the trouble with Groombridge is that most of it is in Kent, and this includes Groombridge Place. However, in the little Sussex bit there is a handsome small house on the main road, called 'Pollies Hall', with an oast adjoining. The church is by Norman Shaw, the influential architect who led a revolt against the High Victorian style in the 1870s and after. He also did Glen Andred (1867), half a mile south, very Sussex rustic with lots of tile-hanging.

A weather-beaten sandstone milepost on the west side of the A264 has the inscription 'IV to Tunbridge Wells' — a piece of evidence of the Tunbridge Wells to Maresfield turnpike road, established in 1766 (see *Wych Cross*). [6]

GUESTLING

There was a time when industry flourished in the Sussex countryside; there are references in this book to Wealden iron and to gunpowder-making, for instance. Today there is little except farming, but in the parish of Guestling, down Fourteen Acre Lane, you can find an industry well suited to its environment — handmade bricks. Hastings Brickworks has its own claypit and a team of specialists, the fastest of whom can turn out 1,600 bricks a day. The machine-made variety would look out of place in an ancient building. Here in Sussex, the Guestling bricks have been used in many a restored church and at Camber Castle, while nationally-known customers include Buckingham Palace and Hampton Court. You can visit the factory by prior arrangement.   [24]

HADLOW DOWN

It's strange, but 'New Inns' are nearly always old. The New Inn at Hadlow Down contains an extraordinary mixture of architecture. It was built in around 1887 to the design of, probably, Samuel Denman, a Brighton architect mainly of churches, and has received very little alteration since. The baluster divisions of the windows, and the way the various parts join together, give a feeling of utter incongruity. It is a proper 'period piece'.

Our eye was arrested by a weathervane in the form of a well-characterised Viking ship. It's on top of the barn or garage of a house down the road to Blackboys: it also has a rather nice brick arbour right next to the road.   [13]

HAILSHAM

Rope, twine and sacking have been made here at least since early Victorian times; M. A. Lower's 'History of Sussex' says that it 'employed a large number of people', but omits the gruesome detail supplied by Augustus Hare, that it 'has the privilege of supplying the cords used in prisons for executions'. A doubtful privilege.   [22]

HALLAND

Concealed among shrubbery not far from the house at Bentley (home of the wildfowl collection and motor museum) is a well-built tunnel which now comes to a dead end. But once the building lay more in that direction and the family had Catholic sympathies at a time when it was forbidden for priests to conduct services in Protestant England. It's quite possible, therefore, that this was an escape route for fugitive priests.

The Pelham Buckle is as much a symbol of Sussex as the legless martlet, and the Pelham family lived in the village from Elizabethan times. Their crest

is to be found on churches, towers and even milestones over a large part of East Sussex, and even as a pub name in Crawley New Town. The original story is that at the battle of Poitiers in 1356, Sir John Pelham was one of a party which took prisoner John, King of France. He was only a youngster at the time and when rewards were handed out he was overlooked. Someone at last said, 'give the boy a buckle' and the Black Prince complied, with one of his own belt buckles. But the story may have received embellishment in re-telling, and may simply be the grant of a crest.

'Terrible Down', a bit south of Halland, is really 'Tarble Down' and it got corrupted. Then, to justify the name, a legend grew up of a battle there at some unspecified date, when the carnage was so terrible that combatants literally waded in blood! Unlike the clash at *Slonk Hill*, you may search the history books in vain for this affray.   [22]

HALNAKER

A windmill stood on Halnaker Hill at least as far back as 1540, but the present restored structure was first put up in 1740 specifically to grind corn for the poor of the district. In 1958 West Sussex County Council undertook to preserve examples of the three main windmill designs, choosing High Salvington post windmill, Shipley smock mill and Halnaker, which is a tower mill. The top of the mill rotates, with the sails attached, while the main body is of brick. The sails are now permanently fixed to face the south-west. Note the black and white beehive cap and the warm russet-red of the burnt Sussex tiles which adorn the outside. You can reach the mill only on foot. The most obvious way is up the old mill road from Warehead Farm, but one of the other tracks is a remnant of the Roman *agger*, or embankment, which flanked Stane Street.   [17]

HAMMERPOT

Not, it seems, a corruption of 'hammerpond' — Mr. Harmar was once a local farmer, and the 'pot' refers to the dip or hollow in the area. There is here a disused decoy pond which belonged to Arundel Castle, and supplied wild duck for the castle table. It's close to Newplace Farm which in Tudor times was the home of Edward Palmer and his three sons, all of whom were knighted by Henry VIII.   [19]

HAMSEY

Is the shade of Edward Markwick sulkily stalking old Hamsey churchyard? He died in 1538, and in his will he stipulated that 'an Image and Scripture should there be graven whereupon the Sepulchre may be sett'. It's a beautiful canopied tomb, yet the top and the heraldic shields on the front are completely bare.

You reach the site by crossing a canal cut and passing through a farmyard — and, standing in the churchyard, on a low eminence north of Lewes, you'll have the impression of being marooned. The great bend in the river just here is short-circuited by the (time-saving) Mighell's Cut made by the Ouse Navigation at the end of the eighteenth century (see *Offham*). The church is kept locked, but the key is available.

Hamsey, though remote now, was a centre of some importance in Saxon times. King Athelstan held a meeting of his counsellors here in 925. There was a manor house on the site of the present churchyard, and probably other houses as well. No explanation of the vacation of the site has ever been supported by evidence, but the one generally accepted is that the population was at some time wiped out by plague.   [21]

HANDCROSS

To most people Handcross means Nymans (erroneously placed by Pevsner in the 'Buildings of England' Sussex volume as near Cuckfield!). It's a superb example of the 'things are not always what they seem' school. The house would be taken by anyone but an expert to be a fourteenth to sixteenth century manor house, but in fact it is almost entirely the creation of Sir Walter Tapper in the 1920s.

The owner was Lt. Col. L. C. R. Messel, whose son was Oliver Messel, the artist and theatre designer (see *Parham*). Nymans house was largely destroyed by fire soon after the second world war, and is not open, though you can view the skeleton from the gardens which belong to the National Trust and are regularly open.

Driving along the B2110 towards Balcombe, you find yourself unexpectedly almost on a level with a Victorian Gothick clock-tower on your right. It is on the stable block of High Beeches, and although only a few yards back from the road is down quite a steep slope. [4]

HARDHAM

The Arun Navigation built the 375-yard long canal tunnel at Hardham in 1790 to bypass a three-mile loop of the river. It was blocked by the London Brighton and South Coast Railway in 1898. There is water in the canal at the north portal, but the access is easier to the south, where it's blocked. The dry canal bed can be followed south to the point where it joins the river, just below Coldwaltham lock.

Hardham once had a small priory of Augustinian canons which ceased in the late fifteenth century. From the A29 you can see part of the refectory walls, now part of the farmhouse, and the three arches of the entrance to the chapter house.

But the great attraction of Hardham is the little church, covered inside with wall paintings of the early twelfth century, and among the most important ones of their date in the whole of England. It seems that they had been covered over less than two centuries after they were painted and were only discovered in 1866. Since then, restoration has sometimes preserved them, sometimes destroyed them; but those on the chancel arch are certainly worth studying. On the nave side, angels above the arch look down on Christ and the Doctors on the left, and an Annunciation on the right. On the chancel side is the story of Adam and Eve and the Temptation.

The A29 was rebuilt and straightened some years back, leaving several small cottages in a backwater, where they have gradually fallen into decay. But the road is now usually above the water level — the whole area can become deeply flooded in winter when the Arun overflows its banks. [9]

HARTFIELD

Back to childhood days! Almost exactly opposite Hartfield Garage is a road with restricted vehicular access. Half a mile or so down this road is a small wooden bridge over a stream. If all your party throw twigs over the upstream side and watch them to see which arrives downstream first, you will be playing 'Pooh-sticks' on the very same spot where A. A. Milne placed Winnie-the-Pooh for his immortal game. More seriously, the churchyard has an unusual lychgate, half under the projecting upper floor of the adjacent cottage. Originally another cottage matched on the other side, but a tree has now replaced it. [29]

HARTING

The lofty spire of South Harting church is the only one in Sussex to be copper clad, and its vivid green is a fine landmark. The complex timbering in the interior of the chancel roof is remarkable — so is the fact that you step *down* from nave to chancel, not vice versa. Only three or four Sussex churches have this peculiarity. Outside the church stand, unprotected and weathering badly, the village stocks. A mile or so away is magnificent Uppark, now a National Trust house. Built about 1690, it was offered to the Duke of Wellington after Waterloo, but he declined because the road to it was too steep. Later, H. G. Wells spent his boyhood here; his mother was housekeeper. [29]

HASSOCKS

The busy Stonepound crossroads has been a meeting place for traffic over very many centuries. In Roman times the London to Brighton road crossed a less important thoroughfare which ran from west to east and now lies under a section of the present high street. Archaeologists argue as to the importance of Hassocks as an industrial centre (its modern size owes everything to the railway) but a large Roman cemetery was discovered at Stonepound. [20]

HEATHFIELD

Natural gas came to Heathfield in 1975 — for the second time! Back in 1895 a local field was discovered while engineers were looking for water near Heathfield Station. Several holes were sunk, and the station was lit by natural gas until the 1930s. There's now only one small remnant of the industry — among the trees near the bridge in Ghyll Road (a continuation of Sheepsetting Lane) about two feet of large pipe protrudes from the ground. In its heyday some 15 million cubic feet a day came from beneath the ground at Heathfield, about an eighth of London's then daily sale of gas.

The Gibraltar Tower east of the village was erected in memory of General George Elliot, Baron Heathfield, defender of Gibraltar in the 1779 siege. It is now a museum open at regular times.

Jonathan Harmer, the sculptor who made terracotta plaques for gravestones in many East Sussex churches, was born, lived and worked here in the early nineteenth century (see *Mayfield, Salehurst*). [13]

HELLINGLY

A group of cottages lies snugly against the churchyard's northern greensward only yards from the nearest gravestones — an unusual and attractive feature. Among the vicars here was John Miller who (like Richard Woodman of Warbleton) was burned at the stake in 1557. The road at the side of the vicarage, and towards the psychiatric hospital, passes the old manor house of Horselunges, a timber-framed building with a moat almost 30 feet wide in parts.   [22]

HENFIELD

The Cat House is Henfield's best-known possession. The thatched cottage is decorated with a series of wrought iron cats holding birds in their paws. They were probably bird scares, though the tale goes that they were the owner's way of protesting when the vicar's cat snatched and ate one of his pet canaries! Close by was a tanyard, the smell from which gave rise to the local name 'Pinchnose Green'.

In the church, almost opposite, is a monument to Henry Bishop, claimed to be the inventor of postmarks in Restoration times, when he was postmaster-general.

We've chosen to illustrate a noteworthy example of rustic building, just across an access road south of the George Hotel. You can follow exactly how it was built. First a timber baulk was laid on the ground and three vertical posts raised at each end and the centre. Next came a stabilising crossbeam at the eaves, followed by more beams and struts fitted with wooden dowels. After that the whole was filled with brick nogging in a herringbone pattern. Though this brickwork goes right up into the gable, there's a small area of horizontal bricks under the gable window, perhaps betraying a reduction in window size at some date. Another equally charming chequered wall is at the side of a fashion shop almost opposite the George. It is a mass of higgledy-piggledy bricks and timber; though some have clearly been replaced in recent times.   [20]

HERON'S GHYLL

A strange space-age construction is visible on the skyline from the A26. It stands on the hilltop, and is circular in plan, with a ring of balls round its rim like an oversize coronet. A single-track road from the village of High Hurstwood leads up to a field gate from where you get a good view. It's one of a number of radio homing stations used by aircraft on the flight approach path to Gatwick Airport. [13]

HERSTMONCEUX

The castle and the Royal Greenwich Observatory make Herstmonceux a household name all over Britain, and both are essential visiting. A little north of Wartling a cluster of domed structures close to the road could hardly house anything but telescopes, and at least one can be seen from Pevensey across Manxey Level. The entrance to the castle is almost opposite the church and it presents a stunning spectacle, being moated and built of warm red brick. It was built in the mid-fifteenth century, dismantled in 1777, and remained in neglect and decay until 1913.

Herstmonceux was known as the centre of the trug-making industry. The trug is a peculiarly Sussex gardening basket made of split wood, and was invented here by the Smith family, who maintained the tradition for generations.

The thing that stopped us in our tracks was the inscription on a tombstone against the east wall of the church, which reads: 'Near this place lieth interred the Body of Richard Morris who died the 21st day of July 1749 aged 63 years, who himself desired it might be remembered that he owed his Bread to his Grace the Duke of Newcastle his great Benefactor.' Nothing else — no mention of God, or his own soul, or resting in peace. Astonishingly secular. [23]

HEYSHOTT

Richard Cobden earned undying fame, at least in history books, for his battle to reform the Victorian corn laws. He was born at Dunford Farm here, on June 3, 1804. He was a regular worshipper in the church, in which the pew where he regularly sat is marked by a small metal tablet, not too easy to see. The Anti-Corn-Law League, of which he was leader in the 1840s, owed much to his oratory, mostly learnt in textile-trade Manchester. The Cobden Club is nearby. There's some fifteenth or early sixteenth century glass in the north aisle window, which has a remarkable history. It was originally in a window of the church before a restoration was undertaken in 1855. It was then acquired by a Mr. Clare in Midhurst. He gave four pieces to a Mrs. Wheeler, who in turn left them in her will to Mrs. Cobden Unwin (Richard Cobden's daughter). She had them placed back in the church as they now are, in 1912. It seems odd to us of the 1980s to give bits of glass in your will, but thanks be that Mrs. Wheeler did. We are indebted to the church guide for the story. [8]

HICKSTEAD

Another world-famous name, this time as the home of the All-England Show Jumping Ground. Yet it has several interesting houses. North of the show ground is Hickstead Place, whose roof has unusual stepped gable ends. The south face of the house, blank except for a small door, is well seen from the public footpath adjoining the show ground (signposted from the A23). Quite close to the house is the so-called 'castle' which must have been a large garden pavilion, though it boasts two storeys.

Further north, the Old Post Office is now a private residence, but in the central brick pier is one of the very few remaining letter-boxes carrying Queen Victoria's cypher. Just north of the turn-off to Twineham is a tiny cottage, Quinces, with very low windows and house-leeks growing on the roof. In old Sussex folklore, house-leeks on the roof were a sure safeguard against lightning.   [11]

HIGH SALVINGTON

The mill was the first in England to be insured against fire and still shows a beam dated 1774 and the insurance company's firemark. It's of the 'post-and-socket' type — suspended on a post and turned into the wind by means of a tailpole — and it's said to be so well balanced that a former miller's daughter could turn its 150 tons single-handed.

John Selden was born in a nearby cottage which was shamefully demolished in 1956. One of the county's most distinguished sons, he was born of humble parents in 1584, yet went to Oxford, was called to the Bar, became the most learned lawyer of his time and was a fearless defender of freedom in the Stuart period.   [19]

HOLTYE

A prominent sign by the A264, three hundred yards east of the White Horse Inn, directs you along a footpath to a stretch of Roman road. Holtye lay on the London-Lewes way (see *Adversane*).

An excavation cleared a hundred yards of it in 1930 and the grooves cut by the iron tyres of wagons could then be clearly seen. This was an early route, and iron slag from the foundries along the line of it was used for the metalling. This would have been pounded and watered until it rusted into a solid concrete-like mass.

A slight hollow running at an angle across the surface marks the course of a stream. A short stretch of the road is on view, maintained by the Sussex Archaeological Trust.   [5]

HOOE

One of the quietest places in East Sussex, blessed with a wonderful view across the marshes. The church lies at the end of a long and very narrow road. Inside is an excellent example of stone supports for a rood screen (see *Introduction*).

Just on the nave side of the chancel arch, in the north and south walls, are two plain brackets, technically called corbels. These would have supported a heavy wooden beam right across the church. It would have been wide enough to walk along, perhaps with some extra flooring; and in the south wall you can see blocked doors to the rood staircase at both ground and upper levels. At ground floor level is a small piscina or water basin with a drainhole, showing that in the past an altar stood here.   [23]

HORAM

It was the Romans who introduced wine making to Britain (and there are traces of their vineyards at East Dean near Chichester and at Cissbury Ring) but its dramatic revival in recent years is almost entirely due to the pioneering work of Jack Ward and Ian Howie at Horam.

Their Merrydown company is now quoted on the Stock Exchange, but it began in a very small way with cider making on a 50 year old press in the garage of Ward's home. Later they planted a vineyard and, apart from making their own wine, set up co-operative facilities for all the many small growers who were starting up.

In a seven year period the amount of fruit received for pressing from all over England rose from five to a hundred tons. Tours are arranged for the public.   [22]

HORSTED KEYNES

Was Henry Pigott really buried nine months before he was born? A monument on the south (right-hand) side of the chancel makes it seem so. It recounts that Henry was born on December 30, 1715, and that the poor mite was buried on March 7, 1715. But in those times the year number changed at the end of March, so Henry lived for two months and perhaps a few days over.

On the north side of the chancel is a little monument to a thirteenth century knight, always called 'the Crusader'. It is only 27 inches long, and the usual explanation is that if a knight was killed on a Crusade, his body was buried where he died, but his heart would be sent back to rest in England. Heart-burials are not common, and this effigy is probably the best in our county.

An unmade track west of the church leads shortly to a field gate (locked at weekends — it is unsuitable for cars anyway) just past which you can see part of the old, now dry, moat which surrounds the church. A little before the gate a track leads downhill for half a mile or so to a large expanse of water. This is one of a chain of hammerponds for the Sussex iron industry. The furnace was situated in the dip in the road from the village to Horsted Keynes station. The outflow is a small stream, apparently nameless, which joins the Ouse lower down. It passes the track of the Bluebell Railway (see *Sheffield Park*).   [12]

HOUGHTON

The best approach is from the roundabout near the top of Bury Hill and down the B2139 towards Storrington. Staring from straight ahead of you are some great gouges out of the Downs, where in days past chalk was dug and lime made. Under these scars lies the fascinating Chalkpits Museum, entered at the side of the Amberley station car park. It's at the other end from the village of a long causeway built to avoid the winter floods which inundate the flattest section of the Arun valley, beginning at the foot of Houghton Hill.

The vast open air museum contains specimens of old buses, trams and railway engines as well as the well-preserved kilns. Through the summer a range of demonstrations and events is programmed, and blacksmiths, potters and other craftsmen are at work, eager to be watched and questioned.

In the village are several attractive houses, including Old Farm, on the corner of the Bury road, and the George and Dragon pub, which is very quaint indeed. But the nicest are down a little cul-de-sac lane on the other side of the road from Old Farm. The George and Dragon was already an old inn in 1651, when it is recorded that Charles the Second, while fleeing for his life after the Battle of Worcester, stopped here for a little refreshment. More recently, a resident of Houghton for years was Arthur Rackham, the artist and delightful illustrator of books for children and grown-ups.   [18]

HUNSTON

The Chichester canal takes a sharp right-hand bend here on its way to the yacht basin at Birdham. Originally it headed eastwards through North Mundham, then south of Barnham until it reached the river Arun near Ford. The advent of the railways killed it, but it had had many prosperous years since its construction in 1824.

The church has an unusual dedication, to St. Leodegarius, a bishop of Autun in France in the seventh century, who was martyred with horrible cruelty, having both eyes and tongue plucked out. Only five churches in England are dedicated to him, this being the only one in Sussex. His name can be shortened to St. Leger: but the name of the horse race comes from a Colonel St. Leger in the eighteenth century.   [25]

HURST GREEN

The church was built of red brick in 1882, its most impressive feature being the high campanile, or bell tower. If you enjoy overgrown churchyards with large and solid monuments, this is the place for you. The memorial we found most affecting amid all the marble, however, was a simple wooden cross no more than two feet high. It has 'Charles Burgess aged 70' on the cross-piece and, scratched diagonally above and below, 'Died Jan 22 1948'.   [15]

HURSTPIERPOINT

'Bedlam Street' may seem a queer name for what is now little more than a farm track. This one leads off the Brighton road a little south of the village. 'Bedlam', or 'Bethlehem', was the name given from the mid-sixteenth century to an asylum for the insane. It derives from the Hospital of St. Mary of Bethlehem, one of the first such institutions, which was roughly on the site now occupied by Liverpool Street Station in London.

At the far end of this street is a house, now residential, known as the Pest House. 'Pest' in this sense meant an infectious disease, especially the plague, and 'pest house' was what we should now call an isolation hospital. Probably these two buildings originally formed part of the staff houses of nearby Danny Park. Danny is now divided into flats, but the main hall is often opened. The monumental east front is Elizabethan, but much of the rest was altered and extended in 1728. The staircase in the hall is very stately, with three balusters at each tread.

Above the village is Wolstonbury hill. The Iron Age fort here is thought to be one of the earliest in Sussex, perhaps dating from the sixth and fifth centuries B.C. It's unusual in having the ditch inside the rampart and archaeologists can't make up their minds whether it's a peculiar hill fort or something altogether different. Near the entrance, to the south-west, is the Surveyors' Hundred — a plantation of young trees in a singularly inappropriate position on the Downland turf. We're not sorry to report that they seem disinclined to flourish.
                                                                              [20]

ICKLESHAM

Several ancient charities still exist in Sussex, offering very small sums to the needy of today, but at Icklesham you can actually study two, thanks to a large notice board on the north wall of the church. These are the Cheyney Trust of Almshouses in Icklesham and Guestling (a widow, Elizabeth Cheyney, gave half an acre and two tenements for the use of two poor and aged unmarried men or women in 1710) and the John Fray bequest of 1592. The money received from this is the same in face value as it was nearly 400 years ago! The notice board covers a space where the church porch once stood, and the marks of the former doorway can be seen on the outside.

From the vantage point of the recreation ground, just along the road, you can look south-east and see the windmill used by Paul McCartney as a recording studio. [24]

IDEN

A roundheaded stone pillar on the edge of the Royal Military Canal (see *Pett*) marks the fact that this is the very eastern edge of Sussex. It was put up when the canal was cut in 1806 and stands on the boundary with Kent, overlooking the flatlands of Romney Marsh. Where the canal joins the river Rother is Iden Lock and the original lock cottage. The lower gates are still there. They were designed to work in both directions, which presumably means that the river was tidal up to this point.

Mark Antony Lower in his History, has an amusing anecdote: 'When I visited this village in 1833, I found in the chantry chapel or chancel a worthy person, Mr. Winser, teaching the village school. I learnt from him that on Sundays he officiated as parish clerk to Dr. Lamb here and at East Guldeford, morning and afternoon, and preached to a Wesleyan congregation in the evening!' [16]

IFIELD

The Sussex Archaeological Collections tell us that the first meeting of the Society of Friends ('Quakers') in Sussex was held at Ifield — and indeed there is still a Meeting House in the village. It was once out on its own, but now it has been engulfed by Crawley New Town. However, it has somehow managed to retain a little of the country feeling. It has had several distinguished residents, but none more so than Mark Lemon, who lived here for years and is buried in the churchyard. He was the editor of that most utterly British institution, 'Punch', during its first twenty-nine years. [4]

IFORD

Very much a working farm village. Iford Manor is tucked away in the middle of a group of farm buildings encircled by the only road, which brings you eventually back to the start. This is because Iford is right on the edge of a flat stretch of water-meadow along the Ouse, known as The Brooks.

The church has a central tower which from inside is impressive, not to say dominant. The chancel and nave are not square, and the tower was built later, to join them. So it skews around as it rises in order to accommodate itself to the awkward angles it meets. The twist is quite noticeable.   [21]

IPING

Bridges are the keynote, including a Chinese one. The river Rother hereabouts wanders through many villages and abounds with fine bridges, but the stone river bridge at Iping seems to have four cutwaters on the upstream side, but five downstream. One of the latter stands on an islet in midstream, so perhaps it doesn't count, but it's a bit of an oddity all the same.

The Chinese bridge, done in the Oriental taste of Chippendale's time, is a frail affair in the garden of Mill Pond House just beside the river bridge.

Round the corner is Iping Mill, well preserved to retain its characteristic appearance. After being a flour mill it became a paper mill; more recently electric batteries have been made in it.   [8]

ISFIELD

Families sometimes seem to invade churches to the extent almost of taking them over. St. Margaret's, Isfield, almost belongs to the Shurleys — and a very interesting family they were, too. John Shurley was 'sutyme chefe clerke of the kechen to or souayn kyng henry ye viii' — perhaps his head chef. John's first two sons died before him, and the third, Edward, inherited. John and Edward both lie in tombs along the south chapel wall, and Edward's has a fine brass. Edward's son Thomas married Anne Pelham (see *Halland* and *Laughton*); both died in the 1570s and are buried in the church.

Next we come to the alabaster monument to Sir John Shurley (1631) and his two wives and nine children all ranged around. His brother, Sir George, lies under the main altar. They make an imposing collection. The family lived for years in Isfield Place, a fortified manor house north of the church.

To the west, beyond the church, is a motte and bailey fort, almost alongside the line of the Roman road to Lewes where it crosses the Ouse.
     [12/21]

ITCHINGFIELD

Long-distance journeys were not unusual in the middle ages, despite poor roads and thieves. The parish of Itchingfield was then in the care of the monks at Sele Priory, *Upper Beeding* — more than twelve miles away. To take services here, a monk from Sele would ride over through the forest and sleep overnight in the little priest's house in the churchyard, so that he would be ready to say Mass the next day. Although it's called a 'priest house', it isn't where the vicar lived because there was no vicar. The east end of the tiny building is all that remains of the fifteenth century original; the rest is of about 1600, when it was turned into an almshouse after the dissolution of the monasteries. Traces of the dividing walls inside can still be seen. [3]

JEVINGTON

'Jevington Jig' isn't a dance: it is, or rather was, a 'he'. His name was Pettit, he was landlord of the local inn, and he was ringleader of the gang of highwaymen, smugglers, horse-stealers and general lawbreakers who terrified the district in the eighteenth century, until they were caught and hanged in 1796. As elsewhere in Sussex, the church and the tombs in the graveyard were the common storage places for contraband; some of the tombs are still in being.

More recent, and to many people more interesting, is a grave memorial near the south door of the church. It is a modern bronze of a fully-rigged frigate, complete with lifeboats and cannon — but NOT, as the guide-book amusingly misprints, 'canons'! It's a memorial to a Liverpool shipowner.

On entering the church you see ahead a small stone sculpture which is dated as of Saxon origin. Many suggestions have been advanced as to the scene represented, but the usual version is Christ slaying the Devil.

No longer visible, there was in the thirteenth century a monastery dedicated to St. Lewinna. She was a local virgin of the seventh century who was martyred by a Saxon heathen about 690 A.D., and buried 'in the church of St. Andrew', which many people assume to be Jevington. [28]

KEYMER

Two saints are linked in the dedication of the church — Saints Cosmas and Damian. They were two Arabian doctors who lived in the third or fourth century A.D. and are well-known in the Eastern Orthodox church, being frequently portrayed on icons. They are the patron saints of doctors, but church dedications to them are rare — only three in the whole of England. Keymer's church is essentially Victorian, built on to a Norman apse.

Along Lodge Lane you come to Oldlands Post Mill, which is being restored. It's thought to date from the seventeenth century: Mill House was certainly built in 1646. If the mill itself ever feels down in the dumps it has only to look up to the Downs above *Clayton*, where it can take heart from the love and devotion afforded Jack and Jill.

The manor of Keymer (or Kymer, in its older spelling and pronunciation) has been held at least in part over the centuries by most of the great families. In the Victoria County History of Sussex we find that past owners have included the de Warennes, the Duke of Norfolk, the Earl of Derby, the Goring family and the Nevills, who were Lords Bergavenny and only later added on the A that made them the familiar Abergavenny's (see *Eridge*).   [20]

KINGSTON (East Sussex)

Driving along the A27 from Lewes to Brighton you'll see on your left, where the road from Kingston comes down, an isolated circular building with a domed roof. It looks like an ice-house for a neighbouring stately home but is, in fact, one of a former pair of toll-houses on the old coach road.

The Juggs Arms, in the old part of the village, has been a pub only in recent times. It's a fine old cottage, thought to date from about 1450. Up The Street towards the Downs you'll see a cottage with a square of flint wall in front of it: this was the village pound, where stray animals would be kept until their owners collected them.   [21]

KINGSTON (West Sussex)

Visit Kingston (near East Preston) at low tide and you can put to the test a tenacious local tradition. It's claimed that the black rocks visible half a mile off shore are the remains of Kingston Chapel, swallowed by the sea in the seventeenth century. In a similar vein, one J. G. Heasman related in 1846, when he was 95, that in his youth he talked to a man of 80 who told him that when he was a boy there was land called Ruston Park, now covered by the sea, where elm trees were cut down and sold for a farthing a foot.   [26]

KINGSTON BUCI

The very thought of being bricked up for life in a tiny cell sends shudders through most of us. But in the middle ages anchorites were not uncommon. He or she would take solemn vows and a cell would be built against the church (usually on the north side, since it was colder and less sunny, so that the faith needed to endure the ordeal was that much greater). The anchorite would then enter the cell and it would be bricked up, leaving an aperture a few inches square as his only contact with the outside world. Through it he would receive food and drink when anybody remembered he was there and brought it to him. On the north wall of St. Julian's, Kingston Buci, are traces of an old lean-to roof, and a small aperture giving onto the chancel — probably the best remains in the whole county of such a cell.

Many have been the arguments over the origin of the name, but fairly clearly it is not 'Kingston-by-Sea'. From the late twelfth century until the eighteenth it was held by Robert de Busci and his descendants, with various spellings. Inside the church is a (repaired) sixteenth century singing-desk with a flute attached. The church in olden days would own but one service book with music, so they had a large one and spread it out on this big desk so that singers could gather round to read it. The flute would give them the starting note.[20]

KIRDFORD

The county's first apple-growing co-operative was started here under the name Kirdford Growers, famous for Cox's orange pippins and still growing strong. In the past there were several industries centred here — much Sussex marble was quarried here, though it is not a true marble but a stone made of millions of compacted fossil snails whose shells remain easily discernible. Glass, too, was a local industry, with remains of a glass furnace at Slifehurst.

The centre of the village, near the church, is a Y-junction at whose centre is a village sign dated 1937. On its base is a tablet on which is summarised 'The Story of Kirdford'. Under headings such as Bronze Age, Iron Age, Roman-British, Saxon, Medieval and Modern are set out in easy tabular form details of the types of culture, dates, occupations and evidence for each of them in the village. A most enterprising and attractive idea for other villages to take up. The residents are obviously proud of their quietly charming village. [9]

KNEPP

For old Knepp Castle see *Dial Post*. The *new* castle was built by John Nash in 1809 but was burnt out in 1904. It was, unexpectedly, rebuilt just as it had been, with a range of fittings culled from various places. The house, privately owned, is very secluded, but you get a glimpse from the outsize Hammerpond on its east. [10]

LANCING

Superlatives are obligatory in writing of the chapel of Lancing school. The chapel is magnificently placed on the Downs, and is as stately as many a cathedral. It is indeed the fourth highest church interior in the country, at 94 feet, overtaken only by Westminster Abbey, York Minster and Liverpool Cathedral. Building began in 1868 and is still not finished. The latest addition is a superb, highly symbolic, rose window at the west end — the largest made this century. The tapestries behind the altar, designed by Lady Chilcott and made at Merton in 1933, were the largest made for this country for centuries, though they are now pushed into second place by the great Sutherland tapestry at Coventry. The chapel is open to the public every day, and should not be missed, as it's one of the finest examples of Victorian art and craftsmanship anywhere.

In North Lancing, the older part, is a pair of thatched cottages opposite the church, with birds on the roof made of thatch — these are the 'signature' of the craftsman, Mr. G. H. Jarvis of Angmering, and we mention them elsewhere in this book. A little south is The Old Cottage, a delightful corner at the end of Mill Road. [19]

LAUGHTON

The original home of the Pelham family with their buckle crest (see *Halland*). Laughton tower, with the buckle in prominence, stands in a farmyard and has recently been restored and modernised inside. It's an imposing affair built of red and black brick and irregular in shape. According to tradition it's all that is left, apart from the moat, of the house rebuilt in 1534; but it was at a later date given incongruous Gothick pointed windows and other details. The church also carries a number of Pelham buckles — look for them on the tower. Under the chancel in their vaults lie many generations of the Pelham family. [22]

LAVANT, EAST

A neat paved path leads to the church door — the slabs are in fact old grave-stones, doubtless better put to good use than to lie forgotten and jumbled in a neglected corner. The most noteworthy possession of the church is a stone tomb slab carved with a simple cross and, in Lombardic characters, an exhortation to the passer-by to pray for the soul of Luci de Mildebi — it's undated. But, unexpectedly, the French inscription is on a piece of local Sussex marble. The other Lavants are less interesting, but we must record that the Lavant is also the name of the river that flows down through to Chichester. [17]

LINCH

Just south of the church is Woodmansgreen Farm, with a complete quadrangle of stone barns beside the road, and in the middle a large octagonal building which might be a dovecote or a sumptuous wellhead: it's actually nothing more exalted than a dung-pit! The whole complex of farm buildings is remarkable — we found nothing to compare with it in all our travelling around.

Linch (or 'Lynch') rectory is situate at Milland; Lynch old rectory is south of the little hamlet of Redford. In each case the distance to the church is a couple of miles or so. As the church is of no distinction, this may be a mercy for the incumbent: Ian Nairn wrote of 'very unpleasant alterations of 1886'. [8]

LINCHMERE

Here are to be found all the Seven Deadly Sins in a church. On the north wall is an almost unique piece of sculpture. The basic carving is in a hard volcanic rock and is of seven Gothic trefoil arches with seven monks leaning out. Their faces, of marble, are set into the stone and portray the seven Sins. Six are clean-shaven but the seventh has a beard and a droopy moustache. His eyes are closed and he appropriately personifies Sloth. Its date is c.1300, and a tablet below tells us 'It once belonged to a conventual church in the south of France and was presented to Linchmere church in 1906'. Unfortunately, no names of church or donor are given, nor any reason behind the donation. South of the church is a fine view across the western Weald, and a good wooden church porch. [1]

LINDFIELD

Over three dozen fine old houses in one village street must constitute some sort of record, but Lindfield is a really pretty village — almost self-consciously so. It climbs a gentle gradient, a pond at its foot, the church near a bend in the road at the top. Hard by the church is the most unforgettable group — Church Cottage (fifteenth century) and Old Place (about 1590). The latter has three gables with bargeboards, and walls with timber-framing and brick nogging. It isn't all authentic (C. E. Kempe, the Victorian artist, lived here and did quite a bit to it), but it's lovely all the same.

The church has a two-storey porch, a rarity in Sussex, and an enormously tall spire which serves as a landmark for miles around. Nearby the old Tiger inn is now used as a church house, though the old name is given pride of place on the sign outside. A little further down the hill, the Bent Arms was one of the regular stops for London to Brighton coaches when they were pulled by horses. [11]

LITLINGTON

Many people have expressed regret that Sussex has no white horse cut in the hillside. They're wrong! It's not very easy to make out, and it could do with a good brushing down, but our very own nag is prancing on the steep side of Hindover Hill. The best place to see it is at Litlington, on the road to Charleston. Nearly 90 feet long, it was cut in the 1920s and restored in 1945 after being camouflaged during the war.

Churchgoers who enjoy exploring will appreciate the low and tiny door in the north wall which leads to a cramped, winding stone staircase to the belfry, lit only by minute openings in the wall. Outside there are three sundials, one on the south porch, two on the north-west buttress.   [28]

LITTLE HORSTED

A myrtle bush in the gardens of Horsted Place (open several afternoons a week during the season) was grown from a sprig out of Queen Victoria's wedding bouquet. Along the footpath between Hunnington and Bradford farms look for two former charcoal pits, used in the heyday of the iron industry here.   [12/21]

LITTLEWORTH

Mod. cons. were unknown over much of Sussex until well within living memory: in the front garden of Wells Cottage are preserved an old well-head and water-pump. Any road called Mill Lane will almost certainly have had a mill: the Old Mill House here is charming, with lych-gate porch complete with seats, and a weather-boarded upper storey. The boards run in tiers, alternately three rows straight-edged, three rows scalloped.   [11]

LODSWORTH

A small plaque under the eaves of Church Cottage, almost opposite the church gate, is an old fire-mark. Fire-marks, which we note in several places, were issued by insurance companies when each kept its own fire-fighting team in the days before public fire brigades. The first such brigade was in London in 1832, and local councils were permitted to set up their own brigades soon thereafter, but it wasn't obligatory outside the metropolis until 1938.

The churchyard is well planted with juniper, monkey-puzzle and other trees, and the church has taken well to being brought up-to-date. In the south porch is a fine modern window by A. E. Bass depicting St. Nicholas, bishop of Myra. The technique of hand-chipping the brilliantly coloured glass has produced a great variety of tint and texture   [9]

LOWER BEEDING

Typical of Sussex perversity, Lower Beeding is higher than Upper! The gardens of Leonardslee are nationally famous for rhododendrons and azaleas. The Loder family, who live there, have introduced many fresh species. The gardens are open to the public several days each week through May, when the mass of brilliant colour is quite breath-taking; and again at weekends in October, for the lovely autumn tints. Not far away is South Lodge, also open from time to time. To reach the church, you've quite a way to travel — down a steep dip, past a pond and up the other side. It's no great surprise to find that the pond is named Leechpond and the road Leechpond Hill, though we haven't put the implied warning to the test.   [11]

LOWER DICKER

The row of cottages near the Potter's Arms pub was built to house workers at the pottery which thrived here certainly from the eighteenth century and probably much earlier than that. The traditional Dickerware included flower pots, sewer pipes, bread crocks and spittoons.

In 1774 the correspondence columns of the Sussex Weekly Advertiser were enlivened by an argument between two rival potters — Thomas Wood and his former partner, William Cuckney, who had left to set up his own kiln nearby. Wood complained that a rumour was circulating that Cuckney had bought him out; Cuckney resented an implication in his rival's letter that he had 'declined the business of making crockery'. Presumably all this was free, if uncomfortable, advertising.

Though it has two parts distinguished as Upper and Lower, the settlement used to be called simply 'The Dicker', but nobody seems to know what it means. It may be 'the ditcher's land'. Once it was thick woodland, but the hungry furnaces of the iron industry denuded the whole area.   [22]

LOXWOOD

Along Spy Lane is the chapel of a religious sect which thrived locally in the nineteenth century but has only a handful of members today. The Cokelers (more formally known as the Society of Dependants) were founded in Loxwood by John Sirgood in 1850, and by the time of his death in 1885 there were two thousand members, mostly drawn from the poorly-paid occupations. They rejected alcohol, tobacco, secular books, music and flowers in the home. Marriage was tolerated but discouraged as an earthly obstacle to the relationship between the individual and God. The Cokelers ran shops on co-operative lines in Loxwood, Northchapel and Warnham, and it was once commonplace to see the men in their dark suits, the women in a black costume of straw and velvet bonnets, shawls, coats and long skirts. The chapel is still used: John Sirgood and his followers lie in unmarked graves in the adjoining burial ground.   [2]

LULLINGTON

Follow a typically Sussex redbrick path between the trees and you'll come across what's been claimed as the smallest church in England — only about sixteen feet square. In reality it's a remnant of the chancel of a medieval building, but the place is lovingly cared for and services are still held here.   [28]

LURGASHALL

One thinks of a church porch as being a small ante-room to the church itself, but this one is massive. It's wooden and extends right along the south wall of the church as far as the western tower. It dates from the early seventeenth century and was probably used as a meeting-place after Mass, as well as somewhere to sit and eat your picnic dinner between morning and evening services if you had travelled any distance. It's known that it was enclosed for use as the village school in 1622.

There used to be a mill here, but it was in a state of decay. It's now been removed to a new home in the Weald and Downland Open Air Museum, where it has been lovingly restored.

If you 'collect' entrancing village greens, here's one for you.   [9]

LYMINSTER

Here we salute a dragon-slayer! The chancel of the church, with its tall Saxon arch was used by the nuns of a pre-Conquest Benedictine convent. They were, understandably, terrified by a water monster called the Knucker (Anglo-Saxon 'nicor'), who lived in a bottomless pool near the church and ravaged the countryside. It was eventually killed by Jim Pulk, or Puttock, a local farmer's boy, or by a knight errant — take your pick. But if you walk for a couple of hundred yards along the footpath to Arundel, north of the church, you come to a group of ponds in an enclosure. The furthest one is still called the Knucker Hole: it is always full of ice-cold water, and the level never drops because it's fed by an underground spring.   [18]

MADEHURST

Not even a hamlet — just a little nineteenth-century chapel with a group of estate cottages on either side, looking for all the world as if they were guardians of the entrance (though even then they are not symmetrically designed). The churchyard spreads across to the other side of the road, so plenty of people have wanted to be buried here — and who can blame them in such an idyllic setting?   [18]

MARDENS, The

Take four hamlets of the same name, and how do you distinguish them? By the four points of the compass? Not in Sussex will you find anything so conventional. The four Mardens are North, East, West — and Up. Up Marden in particular is secluded and inaccessible, but the church is worth the effort. You reach it through a farmyard: it's quite clearly signposted, but a wire fence has to be negotiated. It has, among other features, a stubby thirteenth-century bell tower, but it looks almost too small for its three bells. Perhaps former parishioners thought so, too, because two of the bells now stand on the chancel floor, while the third has been mounted at shoulder height in a little bellcote beside the south porch. It comes as quite a surprise as you turn the corner of the church wall. By the way, it's worth looking at the timberwork of the fine barn on the farm track close by the church signpost.

East Marden is a litle group of flint cottages and a church delightfully grouped round an unexpectedly large well-head which we illustrate. (We go into a little more detail under *East Marden*.)

North Marden church is unique to Sussex, being a single room (no visible division between nave and chancel, and no aisles) with a semi-circular or 'apsidal' east end. Indeed, we've found out that there are only four such churches in all England, the others being in Essex, Dorset and Hampshire.

West Marden is the biggest of the four Mardens, but by an odd quirk of fate the only one without a church. It's utterly charming: indeed, all four should be visited by anyone feeling in need of reassurance that the countryside can be very remote and quiet yet barely a dozen miles from Portsmouth.

[17/29]

MARESFIELD

Mythical monsters by a busy crossroads? By the mini-roundabout in the centre of the village, just down Batts Bridge Road, is a bus stop from where you can see the side and rear of the lodge marking the entrance to now-vanished Maresfield Park. The lodge is an architectural curiosity of the first rank: look at the pointed Gothick turret, the grotesque heads all round the cornice, and the exuberant lines of the roofs. In particular there is a tall octagonal chimney-pot with a ring of animals' heads peering out all round. They might be foxes, bats or wolves, but we cherish the idea that they might be monsters.

Near the inn is a non-stone milestone: it's made of iron and whitewashed. It carries a pun on Bow Bells to indicate the distance to London (see *Wych Cross*). [12]

MARK CROSS

Only two or three pre-Roman camps have so far been found in the forest area of Sussex: Saxonbury camp is the best of them. Saxonbury Hill lies a mile or so out of the hamlet, on your left up the A267. The Iron Age hillfort on the summit seems to have started life as an iron mining and smelting site protected by a ditch (easily traced). Archaeologists have found lots of iron slag, and deduce that it was occupied for over a hundred years round the first century A.D. On top of it is a 'medieval' round tower with arrow slits and the initials H.A. (presumably Henry Abergavenny). It's a folly, dated 1828. [13]

MAYFIELD

Inside the gate of the United Reform Church is a stone, carved to depict logs and leaping flames, which commemorates Protestant martyrs burned at the stake in Tudor times. Two were put to death at Lewes (see *Warbleton*) but the others were burned at Mayfield, within a few yards of this stone.

It's a beautiful village — the Victorian poet Coventry Patmore called it 'the sweetest village in England' — with buildings of nearly every period and every material. The village sign, in the high street, is one of the most elaborate in the county. Next to the church is the Old Palace, once a residence of the archbishops of Canterbury. It was founded by St. Dunstan in the tenth century, though the oldest remaining part — the courtyard — dates from the thirteenth.

On Argos Hill, to the north of the village, is a fetching post windmill with a cherry red roof. The museum inside is open a few days each year: individual applications to look over it can be made to the district council offices at Crowborough. In the churchyard are a dozen or so terracotta plaques, the charming work of Jonathan Harmer (see *Heathfield, Salehurst*). [13]

MERSTON

Cows don't often form the models for weathervanes, but here's one, on a private house. An odd little building, rather like a misplaced toll-house, stands beside the gate to the church. It seems to be used as a parish room (there's only the one room), but might have been a priest house at some time.   [25]

MIDDLETON

When in 1753 Emanuel Bowen produced just about the most comprehensive map of Sussex so far, he put a note that 'Middleton church is in danger of being washed away by the sea which approaches very near it'. It's now probably half a mile out to sea: the present Middleton church was built in 1849. Inside you'll see the royal coat of arms. When King George V was convalescing at Bognor (see *Pagham*), he came here to worship.   [26]

MIDHURST

Polo at Cowdray underlies much Midhurst thinking. To south and east of what is almost a town are the beautiful rolling parklands which form part of the estate. At the east end of the high street, behind the car park, the ruins of the old house stand at the end of a straight drive.

The house was built in the reign of Henry the Eighth and a double curse is said to have been laid upon the family for acquiring Battle Abbey at the Dissolution of the Monasteries. The line was to end 'by fire and water'. Sure enough, in 1793 the young Viscount Montague was drowned while attempting to shoot the Schaffhausen Falls, while the house was almost entirely destroyed by a fire started by careless workmen in the north wing. So, too, were its contents, including a priceless collection of paintings, among them several Holbeins. Entry to the ruins is gained on most days during the season. There's a small but interesting museum of local relics including engravings of several of the lost pictures. After visiting the ruins of Cowdray, take a stroll up the high street to the village square, a little aside from the main road. It has a range of charming old houses and a church which has been over-restored. But the pendulum for the clock swings in the transept for all to see, with a majestic two-second tick. [8]

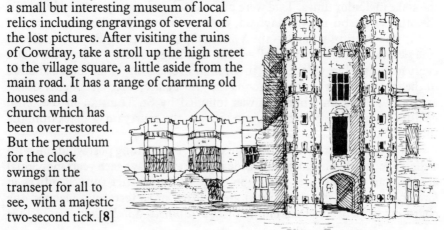

MILLAND

Tales of hidden tunnels for you in this village. Milland Place, now an hotel, was burned down on Guy Fawkes night 1901, though some earlier parts remain, including the racquets court where the German Emperor Wilhelm the Second used to play before the First World War. The original building was the layhouse for a monastery and the monks are said to have made long tunnels through the surrounding hillside so that they could climb to their church and chapel in the dry. The entrance from Milland Place is now lost, but local people can remember playing in the tunnels many years ago. In the grounds is a lake fed by natural springs and waterfalls: Charles the Second is reputed to have bathed here as a boy. [1]

MINSTED

Really only a modern house and a cottage or two — but we learn from the Victoria County History that the building north of the main house is of the sixteenth century, with a typical Tudor four-centred arch. No use of it is known. The name means 'the place where mint grows' — but why ever specifically here? [8]

MOUNTFIELD

Back in 1872 a (fruitless) search was being made for coal near Mountfield when the geologists struck gypsum. It's been extracted here ever since. The workings are by now a considerable distance from the entrance — a drive through dark and eerie catacombs. An aerial cable railway runs from the main mine to another near Brightling, sometimes surprising the unwary with its creaking sound and stealthy progress. The gypsum (a sulphate of calcium) is used in the manufacture of cement, and for plaster and plasterboard. [14]

MUNDHAM

An enormous font — the largest in the whole county, surely — greets you as you enter the church. It's carved from a single block of Sussex marble, and is claimed to be possibly Saxon, although the twisted carving on the pedestal doesn't look very Saxon to us. Still, it is certainly very ancient. The south porch has a group of sculptured figures, badly weathered, perhaps of a family now unidentifiable.

Nearby is a dovecote in the grounds of a private house: you can see it from the churchyard. Down a public footpath you pass the exterior of the workshop of John Storrs, whom we believe to be the county's only builder of reproduction early keyboard instruments (spinets, harpsichords and others). The next field along the same footpath appears to be the one mentioned in Domesday as belonging to the church — still identifiable 900 years later. [25]

NEPCOTE

Biggest of all the Sussex hillforts, Cissbury Ring covers over sixty acres. It's reached by the road east of the huge village green. At the west end of the neolithic and Iron Age fort is a group of over 200 flint mines, some of which went down nearly fifty feet. The line of the Iron Age defence banks and ditches can still be easily followed, complete with their entrance gaps and look-out points.

The fort was built about 350 B.C. and was occupied for nearly four centuries. Then, at the begining of the Roman occupation, the whole area fell into disuse as the local tribe, the Atrebates, were friendly to Rome and needed no defences. However, when the Romans were on the point of final departure in the early fifth century some effort was made at refortifying by deepening the ditch and building an extra turf wall.

There's a small car park at the end of the road from the village, and a breath-taking view. One of us admits that Cissbury is just about his favourite area for a walk.   [19]

NETHERFIELD

It's right and proper for a church to carry some commemoration of its patron saint, but Netherfield's is a little grisly. The church is dedicated to John the Baptist, and on the north wall there's an oil painting of the saint's head on a platter. The artist was Giovanni Barbieri (1591-1666) and it's said that the features in the painting are his own. He was known as Guereino the squint-eyed, but it's impossible to judge whether the nickname was justified — St. John's eyes are firmly closed!   [14]

NEWICK

'Superior yeomen' of the sixteenth century often had glorious homes — at least, if Founthill Farm is anything to go by. It lies rather more than a quarter of a mile down the narrow road from Newick green to Barcombe. It's timber framed and richly studded: it's beautifully kept and a lovely picture — long may it remain so.

The village itself clusters round a triangular green complete with pump, which we're assured is in working order (we didn't try it for fear of the inevitable result). It dates from 1837, the year Queen Victoria ascended the throne, and stands on a plinth almost like a dais. The church tower behind completes a charmingly unselfconscious group. Church enthusiasts will like to know that there is a good Jacobean pulpit with back and sounding-board, and that two chancel windows have an Agnus Dei in stained glass of about 1315.   [12]

NEWTIMBER

Have you ever wondered why Jack and Jill climbed *up* the hill for their water when wells and ponds are usually at a lower level? They were probably using one of the dewponds created by farmers to ensure a water supply for their sheep and cattle — and their modern counterparts could do no better than to climb the steps cut into the north side of Newtimber Hill in order to reach the renovated one at the summit. The National Trust called in modern machinery to do the job, but the structure is traditional — a flint base, with straw, lime (to keep the worms at bay) and a thick layer of puddled clay. Arguments still rage as to whether dew itself was sufficient to fill the basin or whether rainfall was chiefly responsible. The trees on the hill (mostly hazel) were coppiced over hundreds of years, and the Trust has begun the practice once again, producing fence posts and shafts for tools.

Down below, Newtimber Place is a beautiful moated house dating from 1681. The gardens are open to the public a few times each year. [20]

NINFIELD

The village stocks and whipping post are better preserved here than in many places — because they're made of iron instead of wood. There are four holes for ankles, and on the upright post are four wrist clamps. The law was making sure that miscreants didn't get away! They're not too easy to find: next to the village green is a lane signposted to the church, and at the lane entrance is a small triangle of grass with a few fir trees and the stocks beneath. There's interest on the green, too, because there's a village sign and a post with brass plates showing the names of the places which over the last fifteen years or so have been named 'the best-kept village in East Sussex'. [23]

NORTHEYE

An (almost) vanished village whose name survives only in a nearby prison. To find it, park at the east end of the Pevensey Levels stretch of road, near a roadside café, behind which is Old Farm Road. You'll see a large sign 'public footpath to Normans Bay'. Follow the path through two field gates and over a bridge where railway sleepers lie topsy-turvily *over* railway lines. Northeye village, excavated in the 1930s, lies under the uneven ground ahead of you: expert eyes can make out some houses and a couple of streets. Even if you don't find this exciting you'll have enjoyed the walk. **[23]**

NORTHIAM

What's claimed to be the smallest house in Sussex (one up, one down) lies at the northern end of Main Street. A family of five once lived here! Gardeners will know the village for the beautiful grounds of Great Dixter — a timber-framed medieval house restored by the architect Sir Edwin Lutyens. The gardening writer Christopher Lloyd has produced an all-year-round show. A less well-known garden is at Brickwall, now a school for dyslexic boys. The grounds are open to the public during summer, and a feature is the Queen Anne chess garden. A chess board has been laid in black and white chippings, and yew trees are being trained into the iron shapes of pieces set at a fairly early stage of a game. It'll be the turn of the century before the trees have become recognisable pawns, rooks and bishops.

Other things to look out for: on the green, an oak under which Elizabeth the First once enjoyed a meal (she gave the village her green damask shoes as a memento); a lavishly housed parish pump which was a boon to the villagers as recently as 1907; and the Perigoe Workshop Museum, based on an old-established village business of builders and undertakers, which displays Northiam's hand- or pony-drawn Victorian parish hearse. **[15]**

NUTBOURNE (near Pulborough)

The overgrown ruins of Nutbourne windmill don't moulder alone, since there are two derelict overshot watermills on the same property. The mill worked for only forty years before its fan was blown off in 1894, but it had a brief new lease of life as a holiday retreat for the children of Dr. Barnardo's Homes. **[10]**

NUTBOURNE (near Chichester)

Roadside streams are not uncommon in this area, though the little stream that rises near Hambrook is swifter than many. What is uncommon is the barn to the south of the village, because it's generally accounted the largest in West Sussex. Thatched until 1964, it now wears a tile roof, but inside are many of the original timbers, one dated some 250 years ago. Next to it is a round house, octagonal with a superb kingpost roof. Wave this book and the farmer will make you welcome. **[30]**

NUTHURST

The shingled church steeple looks as if it had been prefabricated and lowered into place by a helicopter! It's tall, elegant and beautifully put together. The church itself is much over-restored, but fragments of stained glass in the east window are of renaissance date. The best group of varied cottages is next to the 'local'. [10]

NUTLEY

Windmills always look firmly set in the ground, but they often wander, as has the one here. Before settling at Nutley it seems to have been at either Crowborough or Goudhurst in Kent — or perhaps both. It has been lovingly preserved and is regularly open for visitors through the summer. It's a small specimen, and can't be precisely dated (few mills can be), but it's very likely to be the oldest post-mill standing in the whole county. The centre post, thickly studded with nails, is a sight in itself. For their work, the Nutley Preservation Society gained an Architectural Heritage Year Award in 1975. [12]

NYETIMBER

When fire gutted Nyetimber tower mill on June 14, 1962, the most deeply affected spectator was John Durman who'd been the last working miller there. The business had been killed in 1916 by the Government's wartime prohibition on the grinding of grain for cattle and poultry foods. Within the last few years the body of the sail-less mill has been refurbished, and it's been given a gleaming silver cap. It now forms the focal point of a little estate of flatlets. [26]

NYEWOOD

Bricks — even locally-made ones — come in all sorts of colours, and over our county you'll find examples of decorative patterns carried out in various tones (see, e.g., *Partridge Green*). The only thing which caught our attention in this rather prosaic village was a row of cottages, which in an earlier age would have been almshouses and perhaps are even now. They're of red brick, but the date '1911' has been picked out on the front in grey bricks, in rather big and ungainly characters. But, given the courses and bond used, to do it any better would have set a real poser. [8/29]

OFFHAM

It's been claimed, with a fair amount of cheek, that the first railway in the south of England ran from Offham. Well, maybe, but it's not the kind of journey that we would care to make! The Chalkpit pub was once part of the industrial workings the name suggests, and there remain four lime kilns smothered in vegetation. More spectacular, however, is the double brick tunnel of our 'railway', running under the A275 from just inside the pub garden. Built in 1809, it's now badly silted up, though it would take but little work to make the way accessible.

From the other side of the road you can look down and make out the giddy route by which wagons dropped 400 feet down an incline of 1 in 2 to a wharf on a cut from the River Ouse. The downhill wagons were controlled by a large wheel at the top, while a cable simultaneously hauled up an empty replacement on the adjacent track.

An inscription in Hamsey churchyard records the death of William, son of John and Sarah Pannett, who was 'killed by the accidental falling of an arch at Offham Limekiln'.

With the coming of the railways proper the Ouse Navigation went into decline, but the Offham downhill express remained in use until 1870.

Back in the car park, note the impressive bottle wall — one of the finest we've seen on our journeys. An unfailing supply was, of course, always to hand!   [21]

OTHAM

In medieval times it was spelt Otteham, and Otteham Court is still to be found, about half a mile north of Polegate railway station. In 1180 a monastery for Premonstratensian canons was founded here by Ralph de Dene. But it lasted for only 28 years, because in 1208 the brethren moved to Bayham where they built a magnificent new abbey (see *Bayham*).

The first abbot of Otham, named Jordan, was still their head at the time of the move, and he became the first abbot of Bayham, but as they didn't want to give up all claim to their old site, a few monks were left behind. These worked on the land and rendered it fertile — as it still is.

About 1360 the chapel of St. Laurence was rebuilt, and part still remains despite the wholesale vandalism of the Dissolution. Still to be seen are sedilia, a piscina and several pieces of elegant tracery which make one regret the passing of the centuries.   [22]

OVING

Some good examples of flint building — almost up to the standard of neighbouring *East Dean*. Opposite the church are a group of almshouses and the village school. With their diamond-pane leaded windows they vividly evoke the period of 1839, when they were built. The school was in use until the 1970s and has a glazed commemorative plaque outside in an entirely appropriate design. Two fields near the church were called Bell-rope Fields, because the money arising from their rents was used to buy bell-ropes, but this custom was dropped in the early 1800s.   [17]

OVINGDEAN

Brighton residents and Brighton visitors must all have heard of Magnus Volk, the inventor of all manner of electrical and mechanical gadgets. On a larger scale, he built the very first electrical railway in Britain, along the seafront at Brighton, and it still bears his name — it's just celebrated its centenary. He and his daughter are buried in Ovingdean churchyard. Also here lie the Kemp family, including Charles, designer of stained glass (who grew an 'e' on the end of his name for some reason). The Kemp coat of arms appears on a forlorn-looking roundel hanging high up over the inside of the south door. It incorporates three wheatsheaves, and he almost always introduced a wheatsheaf into his glass designs as a kind of signature. Yet another grave is that of William Willett, who is reputed to have been (though doubts have been cast) the originator of daylight saving.

The church is full of interesting things, including the rich, though not ancient, wall paintings in the chancel.

Haunters of old bookshops may come across a novel by Harrison Ainsworth called 'Ovingdean Grange', in which Charles II is supposed to have taken refuge at Ovingdean before fleeing abroad. History, alas, does not support the author, but Ainsworth wrote well, and the book makes a good fictional read.   [21]

PAGHAM

The Nature Reserve in the harbour was declared in 1964, since when a remarkable variety of birds has been observed to visit it, including little terns, one of Britain's rarest breeding sea birds, of which a colony breeds regularly. It covers an area of some 1,100 acres of shingle, saltmarsh, hedges and farmland. The West Sussex county council look after it, and an associated information centre and nature trail are maintained at Sidlesham Ferry. An excellent guide book to the church, parish and harbour is to be had at the church, and directs you to the Ferry, besides giving a long list of birds regularly to be observed in the Reserve.

The site of Pagham church has been used for worship since Saxon times, though the present church was built shortly after A.D. 1200. It contains a wide range of interest, and you will be rewarded by attention to its details. For instance, there is a reconstructed Saxon jar in the south aisle; the shape and decoration are entirely typical. At the other end of the time scale is the west rose window, whose glass was given in thanksgiving for the recovery of King George V from illness in 1928; he recuperated at Craigweil House in the parish, and he and Queen Mary often worshipped in the church.   [25]

PARHAM

This fine Tudor house stands in its own spacious park. It has a magnificent Great Hall with huge windows and a steward's room overlooking from above. On the top floor is the Long Gallery with ceiling decorated by the distinguished theatrical designer Oliver Messel. In the park stands St. Peter's church, with box pews intact and a squire's pew complete with fireplace. It has one of only three lead fonts in Sussex, dating from the Decorated period (fourteenth century). It carries ornamental shields and bands of inscriptions in elegant Lombardic lettering.   [18/19]

PARTRIDGE GREEN

A horse which carried its master through the entire first world war campaign on the continent lies buried in a small copse off a footpath beyond the recreation ground. The land was once owned by Colonel Jack Colvin of the 9th Lancers, who raised a memorial stone to his faithful Hopit. The family later moved to Cowfold, but Col. Colvin's son still has three of Hopit's hooves, now in use as an inkwell, a candle holder and a doorstop.

Whoever built the houses along the B2116 road enjoyed himself by making a veritable anthology of ornamental brickwork — Deans Cottage, Oxford Cottage and plenty between have bands, diamonds and other patterns to please the eye. In a field on the right as you drive out of the village towards Shermanbury is a disused brick water tower.   [10]

PATCHAM

Out on the Downs, not accessible by car, is the Chattri, a marble memorial with an elegant classical dome (designed by E. C. Henriques). It's dedicated to the memory of the Hindu soldiers who died in hospital at Brighton during the First World War. Though in an isolated position, it's approachable on foot.

The old village lies off the Brighton Road, up a steep hill with varied housing. Above the church with its stumpy spire is an enormous tithe barn, nearly 250 feet long and very splendid. Across the road, in a garden, is a circular dovecote: we read somewhere that it contains 550 nesting holes, though they can't be seen from outside. Barn and dovecote both date from the early seventeenth century, when all this area was a single estate.   [20]

PATCHING

A very old but rather plain church. But see how the chancel arch is way off centre with respect to the roof ridge. Right of the arch is a corbel, which must once have marked the south side of the roof: so a new south wall, three feet further out, was at some time built for the nave. The pulpit has a tester, or sounding board, so heavy that it needed to be held up. The village smith or somebody made a pretty strut: if you stand back you can see it.   [19]

PEACEHAVEN

On the cliff top, near the end of Horsham Avenue, is an obelisk surmounted by a sphere and, along the ground, a row of grooved stones. Sussex straddles the Greenwich Meridian and this exactly marks the line.

Immediately after the first world war there was nothing here but unproductive downland and a row of coastguard cottages. Then a Canadian businessman, Charles Neville, began to develop the area, laying out unmade streets and marking vacant plots — some of which were offered as prizes in a national newspaper competition. Peacehaven grew in the haphazard fashion of a cow town in the American west, with hitching posts for horses, its own unofficial police force and a limited power supply which meant that lighting in those houses fortunate enough to be connected had to be rationed. Hidden among the modern street index are the Christian names of some of Neville's friends and relations.   [27]

PEASE POTTAGE

The M23 motorway junction has shut off the village, whose hill used to be a landmark on the London-Brighton road. Down the west-leading road is the Air Ministry's Upper Air Meteorological Station, from which balloons are sent into the stratosphere with loads of recording instruments.   [4]

PEASMARSH

Tables of the ten commandments, the creed and the Lord's prayer were once a compulsory feature of every parish church and quite a few remain in Sussex. Few, though, are as old as the triptych above the chancel arch at Peasmarsh, which appears to be original plaster and to date from the reign of Elizabeth the First. The church is a long way from the village in a beautiful, if windswept, setting: an earlier community may have been wiped out by the Black Death.

In 'The Worthies of Sussex' (1865) the life is recounted of William Pattison, born here in 1706. He became addicted to poetry, got himself to Cambridge University, upset everyone there, and died at the age of 21. The judgement on him by M. A. Lower was: 'From the extreme licentiousness of his poetry the world was a gainer by his death, and Sussex can take little credit to herself for having given him birth.' But that was Victorian sentiment; we've managed to read some of his poetry, and it seems pretty mild these days. [15]

PENHURST

To come across Penhurst without warning is an unforgettable experience. In a thinly populated part of East Sussex, at a place where two very minor roads meet, is what has been described as 'a rare and exquisite manorial group' — a sixteenth century manor house on the site of a much older one, a fourteenth century church, and a few farm buildings. This is all, and the sight is dramatic in its simplicity. Let's quote again, from Barbara Willard: 'This is the intensest countryside for miles — turned in upon itself, separate, pinned to the past, silent, undisturbed; as country should be'. This was also iron industry country, and the road running down to the old forge was built by Lord Ashburnham for the use of his tenants. [14/23]

PETT

When in September 1804 England was awaiting an invasion by Napoleon's forces, one Lt.-Col. John Brown conceived the idea of a kind of moat as a defence barrier. It would run from Shorncliffe in Kent to the Rother at Rye. Later it was extended west to Cliff End, the coastal strip next to Pett village. Pitt's government rushed the scheme through and appointed the distinguished engineer Sir John Rennie as controller. It was hardly finished before its uselessness became obvious: it was ridiculous to imagine that the French forces, after crossing the Rhine, the Danube and the Channel would be thwarted by a canal less than thirty feet wide! Gun turrets planned along its length were never executed. From the Cliff End Road leading east you can see the westernmost section of the Royal Military Canal, which is more than a curiosity — it's unique, an engineering 'folly' dreamed up by a whole government at a cost of £200,000. [24]

PETWORTH

Time was once when even lamp standards were designed by architects! At the junction of North Street and East Street is a fine cast iron example designed by Sir Charles Barry, architect of the Houses of Parliament, in 1851.

The Petworth estate needs no description by us, but underneath the old fire-engine house is the finest ice-house in Sussex, comprising three large chambers about 30 feet deep. The art collections in the house are superb, and so is the series of Sussex iron fire-backs, the best anywhere.

[9]

PEVENSEY

Here, tradition says, William of Normandy landed in England before the Battle of Hastings, though the great harbour silted up long ago, leaving Pevensey inland. The name probably means 'the island of Pefe', and it was on an island that the Roman fortress of Anderida was built — mounds are rare in this flat region, but the castle is on one of them. The name Pevensey dates from A.D. 792, and it appears in the Bayeux tapestry.

The town was enough of a medieval commercial centre even to mint its own currency. Coinage was first minted here in Norman times (about 1080), and the name of one moneyer, Jelfhen Pefns, has survived. His first name is an old version of Johann, his second a contraction of 'Pevensey', so he was really 'John of Pevensey'. On the site of the former mint stands the fourteenth century Old Mint House, with a remarkable roof visible from across the street. A central gable facing the road is flanked by lateral gables parallel to it.

Down the main street is the Court House, said to be the smallest town hall in England. A tablet on the front tells you its history. [23]

PICKHURST

Glass-making was an important trade in the thirteenth century, introduced from the continent by French and Dutch settlers, first in Surrey and later in West Sussex. But Pickhurst was the site of an earlier settler, as here was the first English glass factory to be authenticated: by 1240 he was making glass for Westminster Abbey. Dozens of glass-making sites have been found, and you can sometimes locate a site from fragments of broken glass on the ground.

Shillinglee Park looks like a splendid Palladian country house, but unhappily it was burnt out during the second world war. The front looks as good as new.   [2]

PIDDINGHOE

Rudyard Kipling was taken with the large gilded fish weathervane which has been atop the church for at least a century and was repaired in 1980. His poem 'Sussex' (published in 1902) contains the fanciful line:

Where windy Piddinghoe's begilded dolphin veers

Unluckily for Kipling, we're told it isn't a dolphin but a salmon trout.

Modern stained glass windows in churches aren't all that common. Piddinghoe has one, donated in 1983 in memory of Dr. Elizabeth Holmes who lived in the village for some years, and designed by Marguerite Douglas-Thompson. Its theme is the movement from darkness to light around a jewel-like centre.

The church has one of the county's three Norman round towers, the others being at Lewes (St. Michael's) and Southease. Walk round the back of the tower and you'll see that the north wall of the churchyard is almost on the edge of the river Ouse, which is quite wide here, sweeps round in a majestic curve to provide a lovely view and has a remarkable rise and fall of about 25 feet. (Because the valley was regularly flooded, the banks have been substantially raised.) If from this point you look back at the church, you'll see the prodigious expanse of roof from the nave ridge right down to within a few feet of the ground in one uninterrupted straight sweep.

In the grounds of Kiln Cottage to the north is the last bottle-shaped brick-built kiln in Sussex — and the only one to survive anywhere in the county. It's all that remains of a former brickworks, most of which now lies under the road bypassing the village. The kiln, last operated in 1912, was dismantled and painstakingly rebuilt in 1980.

A final word about something you *can't* see. When Edith Croft died in 1863 at the age of 13 weeks the family provided a fund in her memory. The bequest, known as 'Little Edith's Treat', still provides an income which goes towards a treat for the village children.   [27]

PILTDOWN

The Lamb Inn used to be the 'local' for Piltdowners, until along came Mr. Charles Dawson, a respected lawyer and amateur archaeologist, in 1912, with his exciting announcement of the discovery of an early ape-man, long known as Piltdown Man. So the Lamb became The Piltdown Man, and its signboard is still a picture of a primitive creature, despite subsequent events.

The story, though well-known, bears summarising, as it's as good a bit of Hidden Sussex as you'll ever get. In a sensational address delivered to the Geological Society on 18 December 1912, Dawson told how, in exploring the ancient gravel beds of the Ouse, he had stumbled across some fragments of bone. Further researches enabled him to reconstruct an early man, providing a much-improved picture of the stage in Man's development half a million years ago. And there was the skull to prove it.

Then Dawson died in 1916, and the next year the 'Barcombe Mills skull' was deposited in the British Museum. In 1938 a memorial stone was unveiled in the gravel pit before a distinguished company. Everyone accepted Piltdown Man.

However, archaeology does not rest, and during the next twelve years a few disturbing discoveries had been made which opened the way for fresh investigation. Eventually by the early 1950s sophisticated chemical and radiographic tests of a kind which Dawson could not have anticipated showed conclusively that the bones were a forgery and that Piltdown Man had never existed. The biggest hoax ever attempted in archaeology had worked for over forty years. J. S. Weiner was a member of the investigating team, and in 1955 he wrote a book called 'The Piltdown Forgery' in which he wrote of the duped experts of 1912 that 'those who took part in the excavation at Piltdown had been the victims of an elaborate and inexplicable deception'. But no-one is ever likely to know for certain whether Dawson was the perpetrator or the victim. [12]

PLAISTOW

The village pond presents an interesting puzzle we haven't been able to solve. It lies a hundred yards or so along the Loxwood road and is protected by white posts and rails, in the centre of which is a bay with stone steps down to the water. Further along is a slope which clearly was in the past the watering-place for local horses. But why the steps? They're too narrow for fishing, and the pond is too small for boating parties. However, we found that the pond water is piped under the infants' school, so the pond could once have been bigger, and rowboats or punts could have given Plaistow folk much pleasure. Perhaps a little more detective work is needed in Hidden Plaistow. [2]

PLAYDEN

A Flemish brewer is buried at Playden. We know his trade because a black stone slab of around 1530 in the north aisle bears incised drawings of two casks and a crossed mashstick and fork. The inscription reads: 'Hier is begraven Cornelis Roetmans bidt voer de ziele' ('Here is buried Cornelis Roetmans, pray for his soul'). The stone is thought to be of carboniferous limestone imported from the Liège area. An informative church booklet tells us that the incisions were originally inlaid with brass, and that this was still there in 1871. It isn't now.

The outside wall is heavily buttressed at the south-east end, and one sees why when walking down the south aisle. One of the arches is pressing down so heavily on its pillar that it has shifted to one side and overlaps it.

There's a small private folk museum, showing agricultural and farmhouse implements, at the house called Cherries.   [16]

PLUMPTON

Climb a footpath opposite the agricultural college and, high on the Downs, you'll reach one of the best known Bronze Age settlements in the country. The area, where there are many tumuli, is known as Plumpton Plain. Ancient trackways run between embanked enclosures, while to the south traces of a field system exist, which may have been connected with the settlement.

Down below, a Norman church stands in the grounds of the college. A. S. Cooke, in 'Off the Beaten Track in Sussex', tells us that above the chancel arch there once were wall paintings 'infinitely brighter and more complete than those at *Preston* and *Clayton*'. Fashions, and passions, change, however; back in 1868 they were completely obliterated. Others were uncovered on the north wall in 1955, but you have to peer very keenly to make sense of them.   [21]

POLEGATE

Along Coppice Avenue (next door to Willingdon library) you'll come across a red metal shed — almost all that remains of the airship station built at Polegate during the first world war. This was the transport repair shop. Those with good maps may like to take a strenuous walk to Donkey Hollow on the Downs: at the bottom are the original concrete mooring posts for the airships, which were used mainly to patrol the coastal region but which were also involved in the first parachute experiments carried out in wartime Britain. But ask the farmer's permission first.

Modern housing estates now cover the old airbase, and they also surround the fine tower mill just west of the A22. It's been restored and is open on Sundays during the season: there's a milling museum as well. While in Polegate, drop into Buckley's newsagents shop in the high street. Annette Buckley has created a small museum of Victoriana downstairs, and you'll be served tea and old-fashioned cakes by mob-capped waitresses.

[22/28]

POLING

The church has one of those unique-in-Sussex features that make our task easier. This is the county's only medieval iron church poor-box. Until quite recently it was still in use for collecting gifts, but it proved unable to withstand the itching palms of determined vandals, and now stands forlorn and empty. Over it is a carved stone, which we illustrate (yes, we have got it right). The church also has a survival of its old rood-beam; it has been over-restored, but it gives an idea of what such beams were like in the middle ages (see *Introduction*).

Poling is a cul-de-sac village reached only from the A27. About 200 yards from the main road, on your left, is a cottage with two chimneys in one stack; but the pots are at quite different heights, producing a most whimsical effect. [18]

POSSINGWORTH

There are Old and New Possingworths — the name belongs really to the manor. The new manor was built in the 1860s for the Huth family (see also *Bolney*). It is now Holy Cross Priory. Old Possingworth Manor is way down the Waldron road. Part dates from mid seventeenth century or even earlier, but you only get a glimpse from the road. Still, the superb wrought iron gates alone are worth the trip.   [13]

POYNINGS

Cora's memory lingers here, with a corner named after her and a walk, along which is a series of seats presented by the Emile Littler Foundation — giving a clue as to who she was. Look at the front of the church porch: it's made of flints so beautifully squared off that they fit together like bricks. In the apex of the porch gable is a carved shield, not mentioned in the guide books. The arms are those of the Poynings family. The brothers Thomas and Richard de Poynings built the church as it now stands around 1370.

Above the village is Devil's Dyke, once an Iron Age hill fort. Difficult to believe that a railway used to run here from Brighton until the late 1930s, the trains packed with day-trippers. A raised bank by the row of cottages below the hotel was the end of the line. And that's not all: you can still find, in the banks on either side of the Dyke, the footings of the structure which swung cable cars across the gulf around the turn of the century. Then, a hundred yards or so to the east of the hotel car park, there's a large slab of concrete for a third form of transport — the funicular railway which negotiated the steep northern slope of the Downs to Poynings itself for several years from 1897.   [20]

PRESTON

If there are any other dogs' graveyards in Sussex, we didn't find them. But there is one in the gardens of Preston Manor, where miniature tombstones perpetuate the memory of some of man's best friends. Preston Manor house is a late Victorian home of the Stanford family, much involved in the civic life of Brighton: it is now a delightful museum, with superb furniture. The walls of one room are completely covered in rich Spanish leather. In some of the bedrooms are ingenious pulls to unlock the door for the servants to enter in the morning, without yourself having to get out of bed.   [20]

PRINSTED

Secluded it may be, but it's one of the prettiest little places we know, with only a couple of streets and a little mooring on the harbour at the far end. Walnut Tree Farm springs a surprise; in front it has two storeys, but there's only one at the back, with a long sweep of thatch. Little Orchard has brick infilling of a timber frame, whose upper storey overhangs the lower. By this means the beams between the two floors were steadied, as they were subjected to a lever effect by the weight of the upper wall. Very sensible and practical. [30]

110

PULBOROUGH

A short way up the minor road to Broomershill a corrugated iron fence blocks the entrance to a sand mine — a deserted catacomb extending some 50 yards into the hillside, where low passages run between huge supporting pillars of solid sand. This area was an important supplier of sand when (from the fourteenth to the seventeenth centuries) the western Weald was England's major glass producer, but the Pulborough mine was much more recent, providing sand for the building trade well within living memory. It's not open to the general public, but carry a copy of this book and Ronald Denew at next door Manor Farm will allow you to take a look.

In the grounds of the Chequers inn are the remains of a monastery chapel; at least, one writer says so, but we found no record of a monastic establishment here. Perhaps it was a roadside cell for a single monk, which would not be surprising as Pulborough is a natural crossroads.

The Toat monument, a mile or so north, is an insecure-looking octagonal tower which takes its name from an adjacent farm. It was built as a memorial to Samuel Drinkald, who fell from his horse and died here in 1823. The tower was built four years later.

Pulborough is almost certainly the longest village in Sussex.   [9/10]

PUNNETT'S TOWN

Rudyard Kipling featured the windmill at Punnett's Town in many of his Sussex stories. He called it the Cherry Black Windmill, whereas it's actually known as Cherry Clack: it once stood among cherry orchards. This is another of our local windmills saved by love and devotion — in this case by a member of the Dallaway family which has owned it since 1856. William Dallaway, often working single-handed, finally completed the work in 1972. It's a fine white smockmill — which, to add to our confusion, is also sometimes known as Blackdown Mill!   [14]

PYECOMBE

Shepherds' crooks are still used, though they aren't necessarily made in the traditional way. Pyecombe was long the centre of the crookmaking craft — a fact remembered on the village signs. As a matter of interest, we note that the curved inner part of the hook is called the barrel, while the more open part is the guide.

The church is at the top of the hill north of the fork of the A23 and A273 roads — a loop road connects them. In the church is one of only three lead fonts in Sussex, and of fewer than thirty in the whole of England.

The A273 follows over the line of the Clayton railway tunnel. Beside the road there are several odd chimney-like structures in the fields. They are indeed ventilators — very necessary in the days of steam trains. [20]

RACTON

Probably best known for Racton Tower, a folly which we describe under *Aldsworth*. The little church is alongside the B2147 road, and looks humble indeed from outside. The interior springs a big surprise with a tympanum over the tie-beam between nave and chancel, and three large tombs, two of the Gounter family. One is of the early sixteenth century, the other a hundred years later. Later descendants still, Col. George Gounter and his brother Thomas, were guides to Charles the Second on his escape to France after the Battle of Worcester. [30]

RINGMER

Timothy Tortoise lived here. The naturalist Gilbert White often stayed at Delves House with his aunt Rebecca Snooke and Timothy, whose portrait is on a signpost leading to Ringmer church. His carapace is in the British Museum.

Three hundred yards along the Laughton road on the right is a large wooden building, now hunt kennels, which was in the early nineteenth century the Ringmer lunatic asylum. In 1853 the Commissioners in Lunacy made an adverse report on it, and it was closed two years later.

At the west end of Ringmer churchyard is a low stone house with Horsham stone roof, well mossed and looking all of a piece with the church itself. We first thought it must be the old village lock-up, but found it was built only in 1922. Soon after the first world war the villagers of Ringmer acquired a fine new organ for the church, but it was far too big to be pumped by hand, and there was then no electricity at hand. So the 'lock-up' was built to house a motor-cycle engine and a fan which blew air through an underground duct to the organ. When electricity arrived, the cycle engine was replaced by an electric motor, and if you stand by the house when the organ is playing you can hear the fan. [21]

RIPE

In a row of sober cottages stands an older house of so wildly extravagant an appearance that one rubs one's eyes to make sure. It's timber framed, but nearly all the timber is elaborately carved with angels, grotesque faces, impish figures and just patterns, while up in the gable is a stone coat of arms on a bracket. It all looks vaguely Flemish or even German, and clearly not all the carving is original. But one can't help wondering how such a building ever came to be in this quiet part of Sussex. [22]

ROBERTSBRIDGE

There was in medieval times a noble abbey at Robertsbridge, a full mile east of the present village. All that's left are a few bits of refectory wall and various undercrofts which form part of the buildings of Abbey Farm, a private house.

Just along the Brightling road at Darvell, once a TB sanitorium, you'll see a painted sign which depicts children playing on robust wooden equipment. The place is now owned by the Hutterian Society of Brothers, a commune of men, women and children who use no money in their community and hold everything in common. The equipment is made in their workshop, and the income pays for their simple way of life. The brotherhood has its own school for the younger children, and most of the clothes worn by the 200 people who live there are made on the premises. The community is not open to casual visitors, but food, shelter and work are found for anyone down on his or her luck.   [14]

RODMELL

Virginia Woolf, the novelist and literary critic, lived here for more than twenty years until her death in 1941. Her home was Monk's House in the main street; it now belongs to the National Trust and is open twice a week in summer. The access to the church, surprisingly, is through the school playground; you have in fact to walk across a netball court. Over the church chancel arch, high up, are three small windows, a lancet and two roundels. At one time many churches had flat interior ceilings built, and such windows as these were put in to light the attic space. The tiebeams are all level here, so that's probably the explanation.   [21]

ROEDEAN

High on the cliffs, with commanding gates onto the A259, stands the imposing (not to say pompous) home of Britain's most prestigious girls' school. It was started in mid-Victorian days by three sisters, Penelope, Dorothy and Millicent Lawrence, who bought a house in Lewes Crescent, Kemp Town. As they had lived in Wimbledon, they called it Wimbledon House School. It soon overflowed, and two neighbouring houses were added in. The sisters moved out to a house of their own in Sussex Square, adjoining, but even here they were short of space and ended up by occupying five houses in the Square. They were able to buy the Roedean site in 1895 and entirely by their own efforts raised enough money to complete the actual building within four years. It opened its doors in 1899.
                     [20]

ROGATE

In the last century the church tower stood between the present central arcade bays of the nave. In 1874, as it was very neglected, the decision was taken to restore it. The whole tower was carefully dismantled bit by bit, and a complete new bay built to extend the nave westwards. Then the tower was re-erected exactly as it had been but further west. The size of the job is best appreciated when you look inside the tower, because the stonework has a spectacular inner framework of timber (see illustration). The dark seasoned wood exudes a scent which fills the church with fragrance.

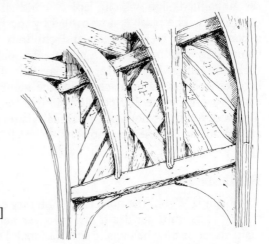

Incidentally, the choir stalls have been removed from the church, opening out the whole chancel area and producing a wide and spacious effect.   [29]

ROTHERFIELD

There are two rivers named Rother in Sussex, but they're many miles apart. The eastern one is said to rise in the cellar of a house in Rotherfield; though the map shows its beginnings slightly south of the B2101.

The church contains many interesting items, but none more so than the east window, with stained glass by William Morris and figures by Burne-Jones. Pevsner calls them 'outstandingly good'. There's an equally splendid pulpit with a large sounding-board and a back panel with huge eagles, all of which came from the Archbishop's palace at York. And there are extensive wall paintings, of good quality, and sufficiently preserved for our appreciation.

The story of the church is interesting, too. In the eighth century, it's related, Berhtwald, Duke of the South Saxons, fell ill and made a pilgrimage to the French abbey of St. Dionysius (or Denis), where the saint's bones were reputed to work miraculous cures. Berhtwald was cured, and bringing back some relics, founded the church here in 792 — though the present church is of thirteenth century date. A translation of Berhtwald's will, threatening dire vengeance on anyone tampering with his gift, hangs in the church.   [13]

ROTTINGDEAN

The literary and artistic associations of the village are endless. Rudyard Kipling lived at The Elms from 1897-1902, before moving to Batemans (see *Burwash*). His aunt was Lady Burne-Jones, wife of the painter Sir Edward Burne-Jones (1833-1898), leader of the Pre-Raphaelites, who lived in North End House. The Grange, now the village library and museum (including the entire collection of the defunct National Toy Museum), was the residence of the painter Sir William Nicholson from 1912-1914. A later owner, Sir George Lewis, made a number of alterations for which his consultant architect was Sir Edwin Lutyens. While visiting Kipling in 1897, Nicholson sketched the fine black smock mill on the Downs. His sketch was later adopted by Heinemann's, the publishers, as their colophon or trade-mark: in acknowledgement they help towards its upkeep.

In the days before telegrams and electricity, a German bank clerk named J. Reuter lived here. He started a pigeon post to bring news from abroad, an enterprise which was the beginning of the worldwide Reuter's News Agency. Later, another chairman of Reuter's, Sir Roderick Jones, bought and lived in North End House. His wife was Enid Bagnold, novelist and playwright.

Mr. Stanley Baldwin (later Lord Baldwin), Prime Minister in the mid-1930s, was married in Rottingdean church in 1892. Fifty years later the couple returned to present a chair to the church in commemoration of their jubilee, and it now stands in the chancel.

There is still a Whipping Post Lane, where a now-vanished tree in front of Whipping Post House was used for tying up offenders in readiness for public whipping. And, as a footnote, Rottingdean was the first place in Sussex to have electric light!   [27]

ROWFANT

The railway has been dismantled: it used to serve a large firm of timber merchants and contractors, and Rowfant Place, a fine Elizabethan house built for an ironmaster, Robert Whitfield. Frederick Locker-Lampson, the Victorian poet, lived here for many years.   [5]

ROWHOOK

Rowhook Farm opposite the Chequers Inn is a fine block, and must have been at one time the home of a substantial country yeoman family. Probably they would have had little direct interest in the object outside the inn — the pillory, with two small holes for the offender's wrists and a larger central one for his head.   [3]

RUDGWICK

The church stands within a very few yards of the Surrey border, and at one time the boundary of the Surrey hundred overlapped. The church is at the extreme north end of the village, with an attractive pub nearby. The church tower is early thirteenth century, and is secured by almost disproportionately large clasping buttresses on each corner. Inside, it is spacious but not specially remarkable. The holy table was presented by Cardinal Manning (see *Upwaltham*), when he was still an archdeacon of the Anglican church. It came from Belgium. [3]

RUNCTON

A medieval priory was situated here, we're told, but almost nothing is known about it. It has some pretty cottages, and a pub whose name struck us as unusual — The Walnut Tree. Nothing extraordinary, perhaps, but we don't remember ever having seen another one of that name.

Near here there occurs an abrupt change in direction of the Birdham to Chichester canal, like a letter L. It can never have made for easy navigation. [25]

RUSHLAKE GREEN

The cruel sea forced an Augustinian priory to move here from its exposed site at Hastings, but Henry the Eighth was to achieve what the waves had only threatened to do. You can see the remains of the monks' demolished church in the grounds of what is now the Priory Hotel. Fragments of medieval walls can be made out in the more recent (seventeenth century) building, while, inside, customers can open wooden shutters to view two skulls found on the site — the evidence suggesting that one of these monks died a violent death. [22]

RUSPER

Yet another monastic story! Here once was a nunnery dedicated to St. Mary Magdalene. In 1840 workmen digging the site of the ancient cemetery accidentally came upon the remains of a prioress and four sisters of the nunnery. They were re-interred near the tower of the present church, and a plaque on the tower south wall commemorates the event. Inside the church is a tablet to Lucy Broadwood, folksong collector; and there are tablets, too, to a number of the Broadwood family, pioneers of piano-making in Britain. [4]

116

RUSTINGTON

On a grass verge in front of the shops in Churchill Parade is an 'erratic boulder' — a large stone picked up by the ice aeons ago and transported an enormous distance from its native rock to become, so to speak, geographically stranded. It's thought that this one was brought up from the beach at the beginning of the nineteenth century and was once used as a boundary stone between two fields known as north and south stonefields. Years later it lay propped against a tall flint wall which lined a cart track between these fields.

On the north face of the church tower is a clock of ancient pedigree, though it's been at Rustington only since the summer of 1905. For 200 years it told the time for the inhabitants of Great Bedwyn in Wiltshire until the vicar and churchwardens put it on a scrap heap in the back garden of a cottage. An unknown rescuer (only the initials EJN have come down to us) paid two pounds for it, had it repaired and extensively altered, and then had it erected here at his own expense. The church walls, four feet thick in the tower, had to be pierced for it. It's now electrically powered and keeps the time, we're told, to within a couple of seconds a day.   [26]

RYE FOREIGN

Cordbat Cottage, opposite the Hare and Hounds pub, is one of the most unusual we've ever seen. In the old Sussex dialect a cordbat was a pile of logs — and that's a pretty good description, since its walls are made of logs set end on. These are packed round with, we imagine, a mixture of earth and cowdung, while the roof is thatched. And the name of the hamlet itself? It's said to derive from the fact that Huguenots fleeing from France to Rye formed a community here.   [15]

SADDLESCOMBE

The donkey wheel, now maintained by Brighton Corporation, which hides in a small timber building open on one side, could also be worked by a couple of men! It was in use until about 1910, raising water from a well 175 feet deep, in wooden buckets whose contents were tipped into lead-lined cisterns. [20]

SALEHURST

It's surprising that a village as large as Robertsbridge has no church. The only one is here, across the river Rother. Around the base of the font are carved four salamanders, the emblem of a crusader: it's claimed that Richard Coeur-de-Lion gave the font to the church, but no real proof exists. In the churchyard are some tomb-chests and headstones with terracotta plaques by Jonathan Harmer, the artist from Heathfield whose work, sweetly pretty, can be found in many East Sussex churchyards, e.g. Cade Street, *Heathfield* and *Mayfield*. He worked 1800-1839. [14/15]

SALTDEAN

Stand on the cliffs when the tide is low and the sea calm, and you can see two straight tracks running along the beach. They're the remains of Magnus Volk's Electric Railway (see *Ovingdean*). It used to run from Brighton's Palace Pier to Rottingdean — nowadays the Marina would get in the way. The coaches were taken up at Black Rock onto an extraordinary long-legged contraption called a 'spider' for the eastern portion of the journey, and the tracks you see were the foundations for its rails. [27]

SAYERS COMMON

Only a few hundred yards from the veritable racetrack of the A23 which splits the village in two is the tranquil retreat of a Roman Catholic priory whose modern design won an award for its architect. Driving north, you'll see the chapel set back on your left, a conical structure rather like an oasthouse. The buildings cluster round a small central pond, a symbol of peace and purity. No tourism here, but there are close links with the local community, and there's accommodation and a friendly welcome for anyone feeling in need of a temporary escape from the world outside. [20]

118

SCAYNES HILL

Opposite the Sloop Inn, on the upstream side of the road bridge, can be seen the chamber of Freshfield Lock, on the Upper Ouse Navigation. A little to the north is a railway bridge, still very much in use as it's part of the Bluebell Line. Freshfield Halt is a short distance further along — when the railway network was in its prime it served a cluster of scarcely more than half-a-dozen houses.   **[12]**

SEDLESCOMBE

A village famous for the Pestalozzi Village on its outskirts. Johann Heinrich Pestalozzi (1746-1827) was a Swiss educational theorist who developed the idea of 'intuitional' education at primary level. He believed that virtue could best be taught in rural surroundings, and during his lifetime set up a series of orphanages in which children of different nationalities could be educated together. Himself homeless, shiftless and a bad manager, he attracted a host of disciples, and Sedlescombe makes it clear that his theories are still being put into practice.

At Norton's Farm there's a museum and farm trail, open through the season. The village pump is covered over, in the middle of an attractive sloping green.   **[24]**

SELHAM

Another of those unusual pub names that bring a smile of enjoyment — this one is The Three Moles. Nearby, up a bit of embankment, the house Hurlands offers specimens of all kinds of brickwork, with the periodic extensions and alterations easily traced out. Beside the porch, a small area of timber-framing has an arresting infill of bricks laid in herringbone pattern in what is known as 'nogging'.

A few yards further south, in a deep cutting, you can see the remains of the embankment for a long-destroyed bridge which used to take the railway from Midhurst to Pulborough. When the railway system was 'modernised' (or decimated) in the 1960s, the perpetrators took good care it could never be reinstated.

More seriously, the little parish church along the Ambersham road has an unexpectedly powerful Norman chancel arch and a contrastingly plain little squint. But one of the capitals has the head of a ferocious monster and intertwined snakes of the kind at which the Vikings excelled. Although of course old carved stones could have been re-used, the whole building shows Saxon influence and must date from the Saxo-Norman overlap (see *Introduction*).   **[9]**

SELMESTON

Words change their meanings with a vengeance! In the south aisle of the church is a brass tablet to 'Henry Rogers a painefull Preacher in this churche two and thirty yeeres . . .' He died in 1639 at the age of 67, so he preached here for almost half his life.

The Rev. W. D. Parish noted in his 'Dictionary of the Sussex Dialect' that 'painful' was regularly used for 'painstaking'. Parish was a most 'painful' researcher of Sussex word usages, and was himself vicar of Selmeston. An expanded edition of his Dictionary, now published by Gardner's of Bexhill, is a mine of facts and amusing anecdotes.

Several inscribed stones are laid in the vestry floor: the strangest is that of Henry Rochester, transcribed in the church guide leaflet.

In the churchyard, just to the right of the porch, is an unexpectedly significant gravestone. Here lies Frederick Stanley Mockford, who died on March 1st, 1962, at the age of 64. The stone describes him as 'Air Radio Pioneer and originator of the call 'Mayday'.'   [22]

SELSEY

Selsey Bill was laid down quite recently by geological standards, but is now a lively collection of holiday homes. It's well supplied with coastguard look-out posts and a lifeboat station — grim reminders of the threat it constitutes to shipping. There's only one road in and out of Selsey, and rather over a mile south of Sidlesham is a branch off to the tiny hamlet of Church Norton (i.e., North Town), and St. Wilfrid's chapel.

Wilfrid landed here when he was expelled from Northumbria (see *Introduction*), and founded a monastery where the chapel now stands. A bishopric of Selsey was created in 709 and a succession of 23 bishops held office before the See was removed to Chichester in 1070.

The present chapel is the chancel only of the thirteenth century successor to Wilfrid's church. In 1866 it was felt there should be a church in Selsey village, so the nave at Church Norton was taken down, leaving the chancel whose west end was blocked as it stood, and the demolished nave was carted off to Selsey and re-erected where it now is — a church in two parts!

'Silly Sussex' is a phrase often used as a sneer, but people from Sussex who really know are proud when it's used. 'Silly' comes from the Saxon 'selig', meaning happy or holy, and there is nowhere in Sussex holier than this.   [25]

SELSFIELD

The Common belongs to the National Trust, and free access is available at all reasonable times. Near it, and scarcely capable of being missed, is the landmark of the area — a lofty cylindrical brick tower with double battlements all round. It's a pity it's only a water tower. But you can get close enough to get a good idea of its size, which really is massive.

Almost alongside the path a Roman road once ran, due north and south. It must have gone almost straight through the main gates of Selsfield Place, the gracious Georgian house across the road. There was a quarry here: you can see traces of it near the house. [4]

SHARPTHORNE

'Tanyards', half a mile or so from the village, survives as a name from the time when tanning was the occupation of the owners. As the process results in a pungent smell, tanneries were generally located in isolated positions. This one is an extremely interesting Elizabethan house whose owner must have been pretty prosperous. Its tall chunky chimneys look well against the skyline. Next to the road is a stone barn: see how it was apparently built, or perhaps rebuilt, on an old foundation. The difference in the size and positioning of the individual blocks above and below the dividing line is clearly visible. [5]

SHEFFIELD PARK

Few places as small as this can offer three claims to our attention. The house is privately owned, but regularly open to the public during the summer months. It's a very important Gothic Revival house, built for the first Earl of Sheffield in the 1770s by James Wyatt. The beautiful staircase is one of those features which gets more than passing mention in good books on architecture — it's one of the great things of its kind.

Sheffield Park Gardens originally belonged with the house, but have now been hived off and belong to the National Trust, and are open most days in spring and summer — though the autumn tints in late October are unimaginable. The gardens have been featured on everything from calendars to TV serials.

A few yards down the road on the other side (a very desirable road improvement scheme has recently been completed) is the entrance to the Bluebell Railway, Sheffield Park Station. The station also holds a fascinating railway museum. Trains manned by volunteer staff who are dedicated and experienced enthusiasts run at reasonably regular intervals at weekends along the stretch of line to Horsted Keynes via Freshfield Halt (see *Scaynes Hill*). The line is another regular feature of TV plays seeking an antique steam train for authenticity. [12]

121

SHERMANBURY

The church is some way off the road, in the middle of the Park. It was medieval but has been altered in restoration. There are box pews with farm names on them (see *West Grinstead*), and a Royal Arms of Queen Anne. Ewhurst, to the north, was the most important local manor, at one time in the hands of the Pelham family, but the present house is sixteenth century. The moat and a small gatehouse are visible from a public footpath. Also on the main A281 is a farm house called Gratwicke — a name traceable back at least to Thomas Gratwicke in the early 1540s.   [**10/11**]

SHIPLEY

An odd agricultural survival can be seen just south of the crossroads of the A272 and B224. It's a road gate and was intended to force carriages and pedestrians to stop and pay a toll due. But the local farmers and other people got fed up with paying every time they went up and down, so they simply made a detour around the little toll house and its gate. The motor road now follows the 'revised' route, leaving the road gate and pedestrian wicket aside.

Hilaire Belloc, the distinguished author, bought Shipley smock mill in 1906, and let into the brickwork above its door is a memorial tablet to him. It's the youngest smock mill in Sussex, having been built in 1879. It has five floors above a brick base and has been thoroughly restored. It's opened to the public once a month during the season.

A smock mill gets its name because its cap rotates on top of a rigid body made of wood in a shape which looks rather like the smocks once worn by agricultural workers.

The hammerpond of Knepp Furnace is impressively large, but it's all that's left of a furnace worked from 1568 to 1604.   [**10**]

SHULBREDE

Half a mile down the hill from Linchmere church is all that remains of Shulbrede Priory, now a farm in private ownership. It was founded about 1200, but by 1239 it had been bought by the Percy family, famous Earls of Northumberland, who held it, except for one short period, until the Dissolution in 1536. The remains now visible are part of the refectory (the canons' dining hall), an undercroft forming the buttery, and a part of the prior's lodging. Inside are Tudor wall paintings including a series of animals and birds who announce the Nativity in quaint medieval Latin. They may be seen by appointment.   [**1**]

122

SIDLESHAM

The Highleigh Pound is neither a weight nor a sum of money. It's an enclosure situated close to Sidlesham Common, and was used to 'impound' animals which strayed off the Common into the village. The parish council have kept this ancient pound in good repair, and it may be seen at the junction of Highleigh Road and Rotton Row. Opposite it was the village inn called The Highleigh Pound — it's now a private house.

There was an old tidal mill here, built about 1755. In the late 1870s it fell into disuse when the land around was reclaimed, and it was finally pulled down during the 1914-18 war. The cultivated area was flooded by the sea in 1910, and has since remained submerged; it's now Pagham Harbour Nature Reserve (see *Pagham*). [25]

SINGLETON

The most eye-catching feature of the church is the old rood stair (see *Introduction*), built into the pier of the chancel arch where it joins the north arcade, and still remarkably complete. On the chancel arch pier are a number of graffiti, including the date 1600. One's sceptical reaction is jolted when one notices that the carver, whoever he was, spelt his name 'IOHN'.

Under the tower, inside the church, is a wall case containing a number of interesting objects found under the church. There are fragments of Roman brick and floor plaster, old nails, and a half-complete Saxon cooking pot, most likely used by the workmen building the original church in pre-Conquest days; though their 'brew-up' would not have been either tea or coffee!

A short distance away is one of the county's great attractions, the Weald and Downland Open Air Museum. This fine selection of buildings would by now have completely vanished but for the activity of this museum. (We illustrate the Hangleton Cottage.) As it is, the collection grows year by year and makes one of the most enthralling days out it's possible to imagine.[17]

SLAUGHAM

A book could, and should, be written about Slaugham (pronounced Slaffam). The village street is a cul-de-sac, with the gates of Slaugham Park at the far end. On the way up, notice a couple of pretty coronetted lampposts, converted to electric light.

The church has several fine brasses and a wall tomb of the Covert family. Richard Covert, who died in 1579, is depicted in prayer, with his two wives, seven sons and seven daughters (Pevsner, in 'The Buildings of England' volume on Sussex, has miscounted). But outside, against the east wall of the church, is a real genealogist's delight. A big Tudor-style tomb (dating actually from the early nineteenth century) for the Matcham family has complicated narratives of who-married-whom. George Matcham married Catherine, sister of Vice-Admiral Horatio, Lord Viscount Nelson, and descended from the Walpoles of Norfolk, who included Sir Robert Walpole. And there's a lot more than that.

From the south side of the churchyard you get a good view of the ruin of Slaugham Place, a large Elizabethan mansion, with arcading and rooms disposed around a central courtyard. Across the field is a public footpath, skirting the large furnace pond, so you can get a closer look; otherwise you must patronise Slaugham Manor Hotel.   [4]

SLINDON

Cricket enthusiasts will like to be told (if they don't know already) that here was born Richard Newland, who taught many Hambledon players and is considered the father of modern cricket. Slindon House has been so much restored that it's of little historical value, but there was on the site a palace of the archbishops of Canterbury, built in the thirteenth century. One who ended his days here was Stephen Langton, leader of the move to obtain King John's signature of Magna Carta. The connection is recorded in a tablet in the church donated by a direct descendant, Rhoda M. M. Langton.

In the church is an effigy of (probably) Sir Anthony St. Leger, who died in 1539; the tomb chest on which it lay has long since disappeared. But it's a lively work, which we illustrate, and it's the only wooden effigy in the whole of Sussex.   [18]

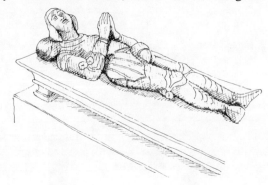

SLINFOLD

An unusual, attractive design of tiling occurs at the house called Chewton, opposite the south gate of the churchyard. Its upper storey has a pattern of tiers of circles, yet there is not a single circular tile in its make-up. Just round the corner are Little Hammers, a timber-framed house of great charm, and Forge House, more classical in style: two more instances of vanished trades being perpetuated in house names.

In the church are tablets to a number of Cowpers, ancestors of the eighteenth century poet William Cowper. Here you can buy a broadsheet walkabout map of the village; something which other villages could copy with advantage.   [3]

SLONK HILL

A battle took place here — perhaps! The Anglo-Saxon Chronicle records that in 485 A.D. the Saxon king Aella fought the Welsh at Mercraedsburn. Where that was is not exactly known, but it was in this area somewhere, and tradition identifies it with this bit of Shoreham, now a housing estate.   [20]

SMALL DOLE

Underwater secrets here. The headquarters of the Sussex Trust for Nature Conservation are just up the road at Woods Mill. Although some of the machinery has been reconstructed as a museum feature describing how a watermill works, the emphasis is, of course, on wildlife. Inside the mill building are displays on three floors, with live fish and bees and harvest mice to watch. Outside is a small reserve (one of more than twenty managed by the Trust) with a nature trail marked by arrows, and nets are provided in one area so that you can trawl the water to discover the hidden life of a Sussex pond.

There's a commercial claypit in Small Dole (you may spell it as one word or as two), rich in iridescent fossils — but you'd need to ask permission for a visit. [20]

SOMPTING

Has son-et-lumière had its day? There was a fine one at Sompting church some years back, but we haven't heard of one anywhere in Sussex for years. The Saxon church is remarkable in itself, and unique in the possession of a cap to its tower known as a 'Rhenish helm'. Unique, that is, in Britain: the design is not uncommon in the Rhineland of Germany. It, and part of the fabric of the building, can be dated to half a century before the Norman Conquest. In 1154 it was granted to the Knights Templars who soon afterwards virtually rebuilt it. In 1306 the Templars were suppressed, and within a year or two the church and its revenues passed to the Knights of St. John of Jerusalem, who made further additions. They in turn were suppressed in 1540, and the church passed to a number of families thereafter; many of them are commemorated in memorials. Not to be missed. [19]

SOUTHBOURNE

The beams of the Travellers' Joy pub on the main A27 road carry an unusual decoration. The landlord collects book matches, and has amassed some 6,000 different specimens. When we went, over 2,000 of them covered the beams of the lounge bar, and very festive they looked. By the time you read this, probably the remaining 4,000 will be in place as well. On the walls are interesting old maps, and old photos of aircraft and flying personalities.

[30]

SOUTHEASE

The church is one of three in Sussex with a Norman round tower (see *Piddinghoe*). Beside the church is a road passing the village green; beyond is a narrow road marked as a cul-de-sac (though it's just possible to turn your car at the end). You reach an iron bridge over a broad reach of the river Ouse, where you have an exhilarating view, with fishponds or canals close by. The day we went, a couple of young men with hawks on their wrists enhanced the medieval atmosphere. South of the village, near the 'Southease' sign, is a second world war pillbox in a length of ruined wall. They were for use as defence posts against the invasion that never came. After forty years, there aren't too many left.

[21]

SOUTH HEIGHTON

Hidden among shrubs about 200 yards beyond the fingerpost to South Heighton on the A26 is the entrance to a maze of tunnels in the hillside. During the last war Naval Intelligence based itself in the building now called Denton House. But don't try to force an entry: the way is blocked and the journey perilous.

[21]

SOUTH MALLING

The famous Dr. Richard Russell lies buried in the churchyard (see *Introduction*). A farm road in the new housing estate leads to Old Malling Farm — private property, but from the road you can see the scanty remains of Old Malling College, stone walls and an arch or two. The Deanery of the College replaced a monastery where the murderers of Thomas à Becket are said to have taken refuge. It's not well known even to local residents. Malling House is now the headquarters of the county constabulary, but as you drive round to the church, you'll see, high up on a spur, a fragment of a garden pavilion from the old house — classical columns and entablature.

[21]

SOUTHOVER

Worth a whole day's exploration, Anne of Cleves' House is a fascinating museum of Sussex folk life, maintained by the Sussex Archaeological Society. It looks lovely though not too large, from the outside, but inside it goes on endlessly, each room offering new interest. There is a bedroom in the attic with a glorious crown-post roof and open rafters. Anne of Cleves never lived here, it seems — it was one of several houses given to her by Henry VIII when their marriage was dissolved, as a kind of alimony (see also *Ditchling*).

Also here is Lewes Priory, whose ruins were ruthlessly bisected when the railway was built, and nearly vanished entirely. It was the first Cluniac house in England, dedicated to St. Pancras, an early fourth century Roman martyr. The founders were William de Warenne and his wife Gundrada, who in about 1075 made a pilgrimage to Rome. On the way through Burgundy they halted at the mighty abbey of Cluny and were very impressed. They found that the then pope, Gregory VII, was a Cluniac, and they resolved to establish a Cluniac house in Britain. Gundrada was interred in a chapel in Southover parish church not far away, and her tomb is still to be seen (see *Introduction*).

It's to be regretted that Lewes Priory is seemingly never open; you can view it only from the wrong side of a high netting fence. We illustrate a piece of the north arcading. We fear that the whole site must be called neglected.

After this, try Southover Grange, in a dip of the High Street. Here are delightful gardens and lawns in a far better state of preservation. The house was built in 1572 and still has the original staircase. The diarist John Evelyn lived here as a boy. Finally, from a later period of history, there's the sweep of Priory Crescent, which attempts to emulate the gracious squares of Brighton, and dates from about the accession of Queen Victoria. It almost squeezes out the gatehouse of the priory, next to the church. [21]

STANSTED

What is there in common between Queen Elizabeth, Aladdin, John Keats and Capability Brown? The answer is that they all visited Stansted House (Aladdin in the pantomimes which used to be mounted in the theatre there). It has been for generations the family home of the Earls of Bessborough; the current Earl wrote a delightful book about the house: 'A Place in the Forest', published in 1958. The house was built in 1686, and contained Grinling Gibbons carvings, frescoed ceilings and important paintings. It was almost gutted by fire in 1900, but rebuilt soon after in very much the same style and layout. The original building was only a hunting lodge: this is now part of the chapel. There are beautiful grounds, and a quite exceptional avenue of beech trees, a mile and a half long, reaching westwards almost to the county boundary. Also in the park is Lumley Seat, all that remains of an eighteenth century classical temple. The house is not regularly open (though it has open days), but there are well signed walks and rides through the Park and Stansted Forest.   [30]

STAPLEFIELD

Staplefield village green is spacious, and well known for cricket matches on summer weekends. Staplefield Place, at its west end, is not old; but it has a fine coachhouse block with arched gateway overlooking the green and across to the little church (1847) with some nice wall paintings, and three bells in an open bellcote.   [4]

STEDHAM

A gateway here could do with a bit of detective work, investigating its story. The church is Victorian, and Stedham Hall adjoining, though it might look old, is nearly all twentieth century. There's a gate between the two, which you can inspect from the churchyard. Over the top, on the lintel, are six pieces of old worked stone, all clearly from the same column, or perhaps a pair of columns. They are carved in a kind of barley sugar twist, and the fourth along the line has a suspicion of a groined crossing. Above them, an ornamental pediment looks like part of a capital stood upside down; and the whole gateway is not of-a-piece with the rest of the wall. They are most likely the only identifiable remains of the earlier church on the site, which may have been the one mentioned in Domesday.

Near the churchyard gate is an ancient tree split right down the middle, each half growing strongly, the whole making a great 'V'. Lightning, perhaps?   [8]

STEYNING

The south doors of the church still have the original sanctuary rings on the outside. Cling to these if you were a miscreant, and you were safe! In the porch is a broken Saxon gravestone, the double incised cross proclaiming its importance. Some say it covered the grave of King Ethelwulf, whose body was later removed to Winchester. Inside the church, on a wall, are the borough mace and constable's staff, acquired as the symbols of authority back in 1685.

Steyning is the kind of small town you can spend a day or a year in, and still keep finding new things of interest. Near the church is a tiny thatched cruck-built cottage with its fire-mark. The diminutive clock tower in the High Street (illustrated) is on a truly historic building, now an office. It dates from the seventeenth century and a painted board tells that 'George Fox, Founder of the Society of Friends (The Quakers) held a meeting here in 1655 (Sussex Archaeological Collections, Vol. 55). The Steyning Tithe Award (No. 613) shows that in 1835 this was known as the Town Hall. It was the fire station from 1896 to 1936'. A bracket over the window is surmounted by a notice saying 'Fire Bell. Warning. Anyone Ringing the Bell Except in Case of Fire will be Prosecuted'. Alas, there is no bell.   [19]

STOKE, North and South

Sussex has three Stokes, but West Stoke is far from these two, so we put it under 'West'. North Stoke is surrounded on three sides by a great loop of the river Arun, while South Stoke is inside the next loop — so, although their two churches are only about half a mile apart, and it's possible to walk directly from one to the other, you have to drive getting on for eight miles between them! North Stoke church is a gem, with a history in miniature of window architecture, and niches either side of the chancel arch. (Look for the carved hand on the corbel in the northern niche.) The odd thing in South Stoke church is a recess on the nave south wall, of unknown purpose.   [18]

STONE CROSS

No two mills are quite the same, and an unusual feature of the tower windmill at Stone Cross is the shape of the windows — they're like glassed wheels. It was built in 1876 from bricks made in a brickfield close by. Like so many mills, it fell on hard times, and at one time the cap and sweeps were missing. The cap was eventually replaced by the one from the old Parsonage mill at Eastbourne. [28]

STOPHAM

Impatient motorists have been known to curse the stone bridge at Stopham, so narrow as to allow only one-way traffic controlled by lights. But it's without doubt the most venerable and beautiful bridge in Sussex, built over the Arun in 1423 to replace the old ferry. It has seven rounded arches with refuges (or passing places) on both sides over the piers. The middle arch was raised in 1822. Vehicles have buffeted the structure over the years, and a new bridge is now planned to take the strain of modern communications.

The early-Norman church sits next to a seventeenth century manor house. In the churchyard is the grave of Arthur Gilligan (1894-1976), one of the county's most distinguished cricketers. The Gilligan stand at Hove was named after him. [9]

STORRINGTON

We didn't find a pillory in Storrington, but we found out about a pillery. The churchyard is down in a hollow, in the middle of which stands an old pump, no longer working — at least, not when we tried it. This lower part of the churchyard was taken over in 1882, when it was called the Old Pillery Gardens. However, we learnt from the admirable church guide that the name has nothing to do with ancient punishments. The pump used to stand outside the back door of a house on the site, near the cross lanes. The house was occupied by a Mr. Dixon, who made and sold 'pink pills for all ills', made on the premises. The house was known locally as the Pills Factory — or, of course, Pillery!

Arnold Bax, the composer whose music is enjoying a deserved revival, lived in the pub for the last twelve years of his life (1940 to 1952). The centre of the village is a small triangular space which was in the distant past the cattle market. [19]

STOUGHTON

The church exterior is plain and barn-like, though bulky, but it leaves you quite unprepared for the interior, which seems far bigger than there's room for. The nave is over thirty feet high and the two transepts are comparable. A huge and very powerful Norman arch has a triple layer of roll mouldings swooping down to three shafts on either side. It's a complete eleventh century church of the Saxo-Norman overlap (see *Introduction*). The Downs hereabouts are particularly rich in prehistoric remains; flint mines on Stoke Down, a barrow cemetery on Bow Hill to the west (stunning view here!), and two five-foot-high long barrows on Stoughton Down, the ditches still easily traced.   [17]

STREAT

Along the Downs between Westmeston and Plumpton you'll find a strange plantation of maturing trees. Their shape is better seen from the road below, near the side road leading to Streat (signposted) — a great 'V', planted in 1897 to commemorate the diamond jubilee of Queen Victoria.   [21]

STRETHAM

Medieval houses in the Weald were often protected by a moat, and you can see an example alongside a footpath at Stretham, south of Henfield. Excavations have revealed that there was a large house inside it in medieval times — probably a residence of the bishops of Chichester.   [20]

SULLINGTON

Another lovely view from the churchyard here, but looking up to the Downs rather than down from them. The church is way down a turning of the A283 outside Storrington, almost in a farmyard, and we know you'll like the old yews in the churchyard. Just behind it, in a farm which sells good produce, is a truly magnificent tithe barn, no less than 115 feet in length. It's built of massive beams and tarred weather-boarding. R. L. Hayward, in his 'Yesterday in Sullington' describes it perfectly: 'it forms a colossal and noble covered space, which, with its lofty roof on braced arches with tie-beams, gives the impression of a rustic cathedral.' One of the beams has the date 1685.   [19]

SUTTON

School Lane may become Memory Lane for some of our readers. On one corner of the lane is Old School House, on the other Old School Cottage. The Cottage is now a private residence, but from a few yards down the lane you can look back and see the big Victorian lancet windows of the old schoolroom — a remarkable survival. The church is larger than most village churches in this area, and more ornately detailed. The triple sedilia in the chancel are lovely.[9]

TANGMERE

Indissolubly associated with the prowess of RAF fighter squadrons who flew from the airfield here during the second world war, Tangmere 'aerodrome' came into being late in the first war and was not finally vacated by the RAF until 1970. Now history is fittingly recalled by the setting up in 1982 of the evocative Military Aviation Museum, housed in the actual huts which formed part of the airfield perimeter buildings and displaying items ranging from Spitfire engines to German Iron Cross medals, with maps and photos.

At the entrance to Church Lane stands a permanent stone memorial erected by public subscription in 1976. It commemorates Tangmere Airfield famous in two world wars and in the forefront of the Battle of Britain 1940. In the churchyard are the graves of some fifty RAF officers and men, and a dozen aircrew from Germany as well. Even the local pub is called The Bader Arms.

[17]

TARRING NEVILLE

Only two Sussex villages have double-barrelled names (excluding Uppers, Easts, Downs, Greens and their variations): the other is Horsted Keynes. Two curious items in the church are, first, an octagonal font half buried in the actual church wall; and second, a thirteenth century iron chest said to have come from an Armada ship. [21]

TARRING, West

In St. Andrew's churchyard are several oblong tombs with nothing to show who was buried there. The reason is simple — nobody was! They were used by smugglers for hiding contraband where no-one would think of looking for it. (You can find them in several Sussex churchyards.) Inside, the church doesn't look English at all. The mosaics of the Apostles and other figures were done about a century ago by a group of Italian workmen with Italianate results.

East of the crossroads is the parish hall, looking rather superior amid its surroundings. No wonder, for it's the remaining part of a thirteenth century palace of the Archbishops of Canterbury. Then for 300 years it was a full manor house and manorial courts were regularly held in it. Now it belongs to the parochial church council. Look out for the fig trees peeping over the wall of the house opposite. There was once a veritable 'fig forest' at Tarring, stretching over nearly a square mile, and you'll still see isolated trees in other parts of the area. There are several in this garden — and the owner will be pleased to show you round and explain the supposed connection with Thomas à Becket.

The lanes in the village hold many old cottages, some still used as homes, but a couple in Parsonage Row have been made into a museum run jointly by Worthing Council and the Sussex Archaeologocial Society as a Folklore Museum, thought to be the only one of its kind. Check opening times, as these vary with the season. Still, the outside is a delight even if you can't get in. [19]

TELSCOMBE

A Grand National winner was trained here. The Stud House, at the south end of the compact group of houses, was owned by local benefactor Ambrose Gorham whose stables housed racehorses, one of which was victor in 1902. They were trained on Telscombe Tye, the nearby ridge of Down, which was ploughed up for food production during the second world war. The gallops were destroyed and the whole so forgotten that Telscombe Tye is now absent even from the Ordnance map.

You reach the village from a turning off the A275 near Southease, along a cul-de-sac road running high on the Downs, overlooking a coombe and offering splendid views. The church is built on the hillside, and the churchyard goes so far up again that at the top (a climb worth making) you're almost level with the point of the tower cap.   [21/27]

TERWICK

Terwick Common is north of the A272, the church (Norman, restored but not wrecked in the nineteenth century) in mid-field to the south. We were amused at the well-intentioned efforts of a local stonemason whose design went astray. A monument on the north chancel wall commemorates Samuel Wormell, rector (died 1719), his wife Mary (died 1729), 'and three of there children'. Apart from the mishit at 'their', the carver found that he'd run out of stone at the 'e' of 'children', so he put the 'n' over the top. But he had at least six inches of blank stone below, which he might have used. Still, he was working before the age of word processors.   [29]

THAKEHAM

There's an 'only-one-in-Sussex' monument in the church, a table tomb in the chancel. It's of William Apsley, who died in 1527, and it has an alabaster slab on which is the flat figure of a man in armour. The lines of the figure are deeply cut, and have been filled with pitch to make them show up. The Apsley family are prominent in the church, including two good brasses.

The church stands up on a knoll at the very end of the village, and it looks down onto Church House, a long low black-and-white house almost in the churchyard, while only a little further away is Cumberland House. This has a brick portico with circular columns also made of brick, though they have stone doric capitals, now much weathered. The roof looks as if it has been lowered at some time. Also observe Gate Cottage, facing the church, and the little group around the post office, further up the road. [10]

THORNEY, WEST

West Thorney is on the extreme east of Thorney Island, which makes it fortunate that there is no East Thorney. The only road, scarcely in Sussex, leads off the A27 just east of Emsworth. You cross two inlets from the Emsworth Channel: the second is known as The Great Deep, and it fails by only a few yards to make Thorney Island an island. The road then unexpectedly crosses right over the runway of Thorney RAF airfield and on into the village. At the far end of the road is the church — mostly late twelfth century, with Norman windows in the chancel, and a tie-beam and kingpost roof. Why it was built in such an isolated situation is a mystery; why it still survives is a greater. [30]

TICEHURST

An attractive village, with some fine and sturdy old buildings, Ticehurst is a convenient base camp for a trip to Bewl Bridge reservoir. The Southern Water Authority began filling it in 1975 and since then as many as 170 species of birds have been recorded there. An area of more than 50 hectares is leased to the Sussex Trust for Nature Conservation as a reserve, and an observation hide which is freely open to the public gives a panoramic view of it. Huntley Mill Lane and Burnt Lodge Lane both lead up to the reservoir, under which their northern ends are now utterly submerged. Dunster's Mill house, parts of it dating from the fourteenth century, *would* have been submerged had the Authority not paid for its removal, brick by brick, to its present site. [14]

TIDE MILLS

Deserted villages aren't all medieval. There was a small community at Tide Mills (half a mile east of the mouth of the Ouse at Newhaven) as recently as the 1930s although the cottages, whose walls and footings can be clearly seen, had no water, sanitation or power supply. The mills were begun in 1762 and, before they closed in 1890, werc able to use tidal energy for all of 16 hours a day. It must have been a bustling place. Now it's a desolate, marshy site, the emptiness intensified by an abandoned railway halt, but you can walk through the deserted streets and inspect remnants of the industrial past: three wheel tunnels in the dam with fragments of the sluice gates still visible. [27]

TILLINGTON

The church is one of those Sussex landmarks which automatically claim a place in such a book as this. The tower is unique in Sussex, and rare anywhere; it's a coronet, four graceful arms curving up from the top of the tower itself to support a weather-vane. Inside, we were delighted by a memorial to William Mitford and his family, on the south side of the chancel. It's severely abstract, and composed of a variety of marbles in lovely, quiet shades of fawn, cream and brown.   [9]

TORTINGTON

An amazing congregation of grotesque monsters swarms around the chancel arch of the small parish church, which you reach by skirting a farmyard. These wide-eyed horrors clasp the roll moulding in their beaks. It's Norman work, known as 'beakhead' ornamentation, and the only other place in Sussex where you'll find it is at St. Mary de Haura, Shoreham.

Half a mile away, in a farm building west of the road from Arundel to Ford, is all that remains of Tortington Priory. Spot a cluster of pillars and the remnants of fan vaulting on what's now the *outside* of a large barn. It was a house of Augustinian canons and was in existence before 1180. What you see is probably part of the church, which must have been an elegant building.   [18]

TREYFORD

An unhappy story of two churches haunts this secluded village. The old church, dedicated to St. Mary, was built adjacent to the manor house, a strange, tall building presenting a gaunt, almost blank, end onto the road. It was built in the thirteenth century and served until in 1849 a large Victorian church was built further to the north west. Then the old church was deserted and left to the mercy of the elements. However, the new church alike fell into decay, and in 1951 was actually blown up. So, as Ian Nairn wrote, 'now Treyford has two churchyards and no church'. However, the old church at *Elsted,* not far away, has been sympathetically restored and has benefited from the events at Treyford.   [8]

TROTTON

Wall paintings and brasses make Trotton one of the famous churches. On the west wall is a Last Judgment painting of the fourteenth century. Hell is, as always, on the left ('sinister') side, symbolised here by a naked man and the Seven Deadly Sins. The Region of the Blessed is on the right, with a clothed man and the Seven Works of Mercy. The whole church was once decorated in this way — you can see fainter remains on both side walls.

On the chancel floor is the brass of Margaret, Lady Camoys (1310), the oldest existing brass anywhere in memory of a woman. It's simple but charming. The other famous brass is the double one of Thomas, Lord Camoys (died 1419) and his wife; the figures are some five feet in height and surmounted by an elaborate Gothic canopy. It lies (thanks be, protected by a sheet of heavy plastic) on a table tomb — one of very few such tombs in Sussex, right in the middle of the chancel. There are three more table tombs, so this is a very well-furnished church — unhappily the rest of it is rather plain. [8]

TURNERS HILL

An apt name for a village whose central cross-roads fall right on the apex of three awkward gradients. A few yards along Church Road, westwards, is a low detached stone building which is now the local fire brigade depôt. But on one end it has an elegantly carved inscription dated 1919, saying 'Smith and Wheelwright'. We think those were the two trades, not two surnames. [5]

TWINEHAM

The Quakers loathed the 'steeple houses' in the seventeenth century, and many were jailed for their opposition — yet they actually bought a piece of the Anglican churchyard here as a burial ground. It's marked by four small stones. The vicar's daughter married a Quaker, and he offered them the land so that she shouldn't be buried in unconsecrated ground. The Quakers also loathed the tithing system, but they agreed to pay a shilling a year for the plot so long as the Church handed over 1s. 6d. for using the grass that grew there as animal fodder. The current equivalent is 2p — and the rector still pays his dues at a ceremony by the burial ground.

The church is interesting in that it's one of three built in Tudor times entirely of brick; it has a Horsham stone roof. Inside is a modern stained glass window showing St. Peter, next to the old pulpit. It's odd, we think, that the window is very heavily splayed towards the east, but not at all towards the west. Seeing the window jamb outside the church makes it clear that it is a later insertion, perhaps to give better light onto the pulpit. But the north side is a bad choice for light, and trees grow quite close. [11]

136

UCKFIELD

There's an unusual Japanese memorial in the churchyard, celebrating the venerable John Batchelor who was a missionary to the Ainu people of Hokkaido for 64 years — until he was 87. He died, aged 90, in 1944. The memorial is made of granite, and there's a cut-out of Japan's north island in slate. A prodigious cedar tree which overhangs it has the appearance of being centuries old. There must be something in the soil for it was, in fact, planted around 1870.

Uckfield's most celebrated building is Bridge Cottage, a medieval hall-house, whch stands back from the railway level crossing.

There is a story that The Maiden's Head Inn was The King's Head until Queen Elizabeth I stayed there and ordered the change: but Augustus Hare, writing in 1896, refers to it as The King's Head. So the story is only a story. He also mentions that opposite it is a stone room, probably once a prison. [12]

UDIMORE

Service trees are something of a mystery, and you can study one of the biggest in Britain by following the drive into Parsonage Farm. It's opposite the house. The Wheelers, who live here, are sufficiently proud of their specimen (one of many fine trees in the grounds) not to mind a respectful visit. The tree is some 55 feet high, with a vigorously twisted trunk. You can distinguish it in the spring by its white, may-like blossom and in the autumn by its beautiful orange-red leaves. There are dark fruits, too, which used to be regarded as a delicacy and were used in love potions. Service trees, related to the rowan, are said to be a remnant of ancient woodlands. Their other name is the chequer tree and there's a connection, not fully understood even by the experts, with the numerous Chequers Inns to be found in Sussex and elsewhere. [24]

UPPER BEEDING

Fully fifteen miles from, and lower than, Lower Beeding — but we don't know why the names were so allocated. The *least* hidden part of the village is the great cement works whose products used to coat the neighbouring workers' houses in off-white powder. But that has all changed with a vast modernisation scheme carried out in recent years — at least, one hopes it has. The *most* hidden part is Sele Priory, a Benedictine foundation dated 1075; the founder was William de Braose. The parish church was apparently the priory church, but all the rest is buried under the foundations of the adjoining house. [19]

UPPER DICKER

Find a boat by the lake at The Dicker and row to the island on which the financier and rogue Horatio Bottomley had his summer house. Near the remains of it, in the grass, is a mosaic of the zodiac — a legacy of the spiritual group which lived here in recent years. It's now the home of St. Bede's public school, whose headmaster welcomes visitors: but report first! This book is also the passport to Bottomley's racecourse. Call in at the Clifton Farm shop: they'll point out what's left of the grandstand and direct you to the stone he erected to his favourite racehorse.

Nearby is the moated Michelham Priory, a popular spot for those who like to mix history with peaceful surroundings. Among the attractions here are a working watermill; a 'physic garden', growing the plants that were used medicinally in medieval times; and a sturdy old Sussex barn. Note that one of its doors is far higher than the other — the carts would come in one side fully laden and leave the other way, empty.   [22]

UPPERTON

The Upperton Monument isn't a monument at all — it's a folly. It's on the north side of the village, on the road up to Lurgashall. Just inside the Petworth Park wall, you'll see a tall tower in grey stone, quite plain, with an even taller stair-turret at one corner. It was built about 1800 to provide a focus for the view from Petworth House. Now it's a residence, no doubt for athletic stair-climbers. Just across the road, in a private garden, is an intriguing black and white painted wooden Gothic gazebo.   [9]

UPWALTHAM

A remote little churchlet on a hillside, with a complete set of chandeliers — electricity has still not arrived. Although not old, they are entirely in keeping. The church has an apsidal (semi-circular in plan) chancel and east end, of which there are only four ancient ones in Sussex: the others are at Newhaven, North Marden and Worth, and all are subjects of historical study. In the chancel is an elegant twelfth century piscina (see *Introduction*). The great Cardinal Manning started his career in the Anglican church, and was curate here.   [18]

WADHURST

There are no fewer than 31 cast iron slabs (or ledgers) set into the floor of Wadhurst church — a declaration, almost, of the village's importance as a centre of the Wealden iron industry. Mostly memorials rather than the covers of actual burial places, their dates range from 1617 to 1799. We've mentioned elsewhere the strange spellings and inverted letters which were quite common during this period. Note here the occasional appearance of the Latin words 'aetatis suae' ('aged') without any figure actually being given: the craftsman, presumably, used the words out of habit without having a clue what they meant — or was it perhaps that a standard mould was used, leaving only the actual figure to be inserted (should anyone understand the language) for each burial?

[7]

WALBERTON

Another gravestone story, but from the other end of the county. The victims of two accidents are buried here, but we'll concentrate on one and leave you to enjoy finding the other. A little to the right of the path is a headstone to Charles Cook, 'who lost his life by the fall of a tree the 20th of March 1767, aged 30 years'. At the top of the stone the whole sorry event is recounted — Mr. Cook on his back under the tree, the woodman with his axe, holding up his hands in horror at what he has done, Death on the left directing an arrow at him, Time with scythe and hourglass on the other side, and God in glory with a pair of trumpeting angels above. Quite splendid! Earl Woolton and his wife are also buried here. Lord Woolton was Minister of Food during much of the second world war, and later chairman of the Conservative party. [18]

WALDERTON

Easy to confuse the name with the previous entry: Walderton is a little cluster of cottages a mile or so south west of Stoughton. The steep slope of Walderton Down closes it in to the east, while north west up the B2146 is Watergate Hanger, where a Roman villa was discovered. There's no church.

[17]

WALDRON

English wines are an expanding industry (see *Horam*), and some of the finest come from Waldron vineyards, just down the road from the church. Fully operational vineyards are still a bit of a rarity, but here you can see the grapes growing well despite the uncertainties of an English summer. You can buy, too. The most striking feature of the church is the north aisle, where a full king-post roof appears still to have its original timbers, dating back 700 years. The village was recorded in the time of Edward the Confessor, and was the home of Sir William de Waldrene or Walderne, Lord Mayor of London in 1412. [22]

WALSTEAD

There's plenty of scope here for exploring the rural area east of Haywards Heath and Lindfield. The Bluebell Railway runs over the road at Freshfield Halt, and a hundred yards or so down the hill is Cockhaise Mill, over an upper reach of the river Ouse, weather-boarded and picturesque. Up the twisty incline is a group of cottages by a duckpond; two of them, white painted, look as if their roofs were inadvertently made a size too large, and had had a curved and recessed coving inserted where one would expect to see the ends of rafters.

Half a mile south west is East Mascalls, a romantic house dated 1578 but enlarged and 'improved' in 1896. A little further on again is a picture-postcard cottage with a front garden well stocked with a sizeable model cottage, a windmill, a pond, rockeries and other bits of picturesquery.[12]

WANNOCK

Older visitors to Eastbourne will remember the famous Wannock Tea Gardens, a big attraction in their day but now largely built over. The odd-sounding name may be an old stream-name, but no-one really knows. Filching Manor, just south, is a fifteenth century hall-type, timber framed house, behind which is Combe Hill, one of the steepest parts of the Downs, with a neolithic camp and a number of bowl barrows where a small hoard of stone axes was found. [28]

WARBLETON

The Victorians 'improved' so many Sussex churches that it's fairly unusual to come across the box pews beloved of their Georgian forebears. In Warbleton church there's something even more unusual — a galleried manorial pew which you reach via a dozen steps. Built in 1722, and still in use, it has a commanding view of the chancel and pulpit.

Richard Woodman, a local ironmaster and churchwarden here, was burned at the stake in Lewes on June 22, 1557, having called his rector 'Mr. Facing-Both-Ways' for being a protestant under Henry the Eighth and a catholic under Mary (see also *Mayfield*). His story is told on the west wall of the nave, and also on the churchyard wall close to the stile. The lane down which he tried to escape lies half a mile north of the church on the left of the road leading to Heathfield, opposite a house named Wayside.[23]

WARMINGHURST

William Penn the Quaker lived in a house across the fields of which a few bits of wall can still be seen. On his return from Pennsylvania he stayed here while delivering a series of addresses to meetings at the Blue Idol (see *Coneyhurst*); he regularly walked between the two, a distance of over ten miles in all.

The village has vanished, leaving a delightful church with a full complement of eighteenth century box pews and a three decker pulpit, plus a chancel screen with coat-of-arms of Queen Anne, all in lovely natural wood. But it has been declared redundant, and it looks as if nobody loves it any more. Even if the church has to go, one prays that some museum will get the woodwork and conserve it carefully.   [19]

WARNHAM

The Warnham War Museum, on the main A24, contains the finest collection in the south of England of relics and memorabilia of the first and second world wars, together with some material from earlier wars still. Here are vehicles, uniforms, badges, arms, ration books and propaganda — even a NAAFI tea wagon. And there's a good range of souvenirs to buy.

Thanks to the local subsoil, Warnham has long been a place where bricks are made, and the Warnham brickworks are a big name in the trade — they've supplied bricks over most of southern England. The Sussex iron industry had a remnant in the large millpond, probably dug about 1600 for the local furnace.

The lychgate to the church is, you think as you enter, just a lychgate. But it's roofed with the branches of living yew trees.

Warnham Court is the largest building round the village; it's of 1828, in mock-Elizabethan style, and is now a school.   [3]

WARNINGCAMP

A tiny hamlet on rising ground south of the river Arun near Arundel. It has two or three pretty cottages, and one house of which the end looks as if it were an enormous blind arch. Then you look again, and realise that the 'arch' is formed by two external chimney-flues, which change direction just below roof level so as to feed into a single chimney-stack. Sussex is full of these idiosyncrasies of domestic building and, as we're now nearly at the end of this book, we must remind readers that there must be many we have overlooked.   [18]

141

WARNINGLID

The village sign, presented in 1967, has a picture of a Saxon chieftain and tells us that the name was once 'Werna-gelad' (Werna's path), at least according to R. G. Roberts's 'The Place-names of Sussex'. The big house, Lydhurst, has large but plain entrance gates reached over a hump-back bridge across a most ornamental pond. Our eyes were caught by the notice beside the gate, which says, among other things, 'No unauthorised or foreign-made vehicles'.

Lord Tennyson came to live here in a small cottage (now much altered) in the south-west corner of the village, almost opposite the post office. That was in 1850, just after his marriage. He loathed it and left the county in disgust, only to return seventeen years later (see *Blackdown*).   [11]

WARTLING

Church lecterns traditionally take the form of eagles, but at Wartling the king of the birds has to give way to a heron. Carved from an elm growing on the Glyndebourne estate, it reflects the fact that herons have nested in the parish for at least a century. There are three heronries fairly close to the church.

On the wall above the chancel arch (and illuminated for visitors by a light which works on a time switch) is a royal coat of arms. These were first introduced into the churches of England by Henry the Eighth, who was keen to show who was in charge, but many were removed in Queen Mary's reign and Cromwell's rule saw the destruction of most of the others. Wartling's dates from 1731 and has been restored.   [23]

WASHINGTON

The Rev. John Evans wrote the first guide to Worthing in 1805; in it he writes of Washington: 'Here is nothing attractive excepting its rural situation.' The arrival of the motor car and the A24 stopped that, but within the last twenty years the road has been diverted and the village peace has resumed. The church tower is remarkable because it's really two joined together. The first church was Norman, but was soon dismantled to make way for a bigger one built by the Knights Templars, including an octagonal tower entered by a door where the vestry arch now is. In Henry the Eighth's time a new bell-tower was built rather more centrally and the old tower was left as a lean-to, the southern part of the octagon being sheared off. So now there's a Tudor tower with the older one showing as a bulge on the north side.

In the parish, on top of the Downs, is Chanctonbury Ring, which has its own entry under *Chanctonbury*. [19]

WEST BLATCHINGTON

John Constable painted the mill in 1825, but we don't know how old it was then. This smock mill was a natural subject for him, because it's a strangely attractive creation, being incorporated into a barn — or rather, since the evidence seems to point in that direction, with a barn added to it. With the mill at Rottingdean, the West Blatchington mill shares the distinction of being marked on Admiralty charts, because it was easily visible from the sea and so made a good landmark.

The sweeps were blown off by a gale in 1897, and that put an end to its working life. But the mill is now in the hands of Hove Borough Council and has been restored. It's listed as a building of special architectural interest, grade 2, and a group of volunteer enthusiasts opens it to the public every Sunday afternoon in the summer. An excellent leaflet is available. [20]

WESTBOURNE

A picturesque small town where we didn't quite expect it: it's surprisingly busy with traffic. But there are plenty of charming cottages off the main road, and a very spacious church. The path from gate to north door of the church is lined on both sides by yew trees, which make a shady avenue. The church guide (which is most likely right) says that the avenue was planted about 1545, and is probably the oldest avenue of yews in England. They certainly look as if they might be 450 years old. [30]

143

WEST BURTON

Not all monuments, thank goodness, commemorate the famous and worldly. Who could wish for a better memorial than the simple stone erected to Fred Hughes, 'who worked these fields and loved them' and which overlooks the farm he built? To find it you pass the West Burton sign going north on the A29. After a few hundred yards there's a footpath sign to your left: the stone is near the second stile you come to, on a tree-covered bank. Fred, we read, 'never wanted any more, only to be free' (see our title-page).

In the village itself is a quite remarkably captivating collection of cottages. The Jacobean gateway of Coke's House is approached by a gentle slope which must have been restricted to foot passengers. Members of the Coke family (who pronounce their name 'Cook') settled here in the reign of the first Elizabeth, and were probably related to the Cokes of Holkham, Norfolk, distinguished lawyers. **[18]**

WEST CHILTINGTON

Squints (in churches, that is) come in all shapes and sizes, as diligent explorers in Sussex will know, but that in West Chiltington is the longest in the county and is a veritable tunnel. Also in the church are extensive wall paintings, of thirteenth century origin, restored sympathetically and well kept. Outside, also well preserved, are the village stocks and whipping-post.

The old village reading-room, down the hill beside the church, is now the museum; it contains a number of interesting items including a flint-breaking pestle and mortar the size of a small dustbin. They were used by prisoners employed on road repairs or other building work.

There's a smock mill which is a scheduled building, but it's not open to the public. **[10]**

WEST DEAN, East Sussex

Whether or not Alfred the Great had his palace at this West Dean (and it has very reasonable claims to the association) there's no doubting the venerability of the flint and stone rectory. The oldest part dates from 1220, and it's claimed to be the oldest inhabited rectory in the country. The walls are two and a half feet thick, and it still has the ancient oak shutters which closed the lancet windows in days when glass was too expensive for the clergy to install.

A conservation village in the heart of Friston Forest, West Dean is a thorough delight. Note the sturdy flint wall which surrounds the site of the former manor house. Inside are a circular flint dovecote (which once would have had a conical roof) and the beautiful worn buildings of a former farmyard. [28]

WEST DEAN, West Sussex

You can witness an eerie conservation exercise in the grounds of West Dean College, where two ten feet high beech trunks, complete with bracket fungus, are preserved for all time in resin, heavily grey like elephant hide. The eccentric Edward James, who inherited the property in 1921, couldn't bear to let them go. Time stands still within the house as well as outside: on the back staircase is a specially-made carpet with, rather pathetically, footprints in white of James' wife, the dancer Tilly Losch. An early supporter and collector of surrealist art, James set up an educational charity trust which now uses the house (designed by James Wyatt in 1804) for seminars and educational courses. [17]

WESTERGATE

'The Labour in Vain' is not an inn-name unique to this village, but it's the only one in Sussex. It shows on one side a buxom white woman busily scrubbing a little piccaninny in a hip-bath, trying to get the blackness off. On the other side she stands back and stares at him in despair. The story goes that the buxom lady was the wife of a former landlord, whose casual infidelity brought disastrous consequences which she couldn't disguise.[18]

WESTFIELD

Over the arch of the church porch is a sundial with the letters CR and the date 1626. It seems safe to guess that the letters stand for Carolus Rex, since the date fits the reign of King Charles. More problematic is the stone panel over the western buttress, which is inscribed I.B.R.R. 1624. It's surely too prominent to be the mark of a workman, however good his reputation and inflated his ego. We had managed to think up 'Iacobus' (James) 'Britanniae Rex', which would fit the date, but the second R has stubbornly eluded our detective faculties. Any bright ideas from our readers?

The vicar, Edwin Wilkinson, has made a model which colourfully illustrates the many alterations to the church over the centuries, and he's very happy to show it to any interested groups.   [24]

WEST GRINSTEAD

It must be all of fifteen miles from the church here down the river Adur to the coast, yet in the Middle Ages boats used to navigate quite regularly up the river to the church, near which is a crossing point. The village is well away, and St. George's, one of Sussex's most interesting churches, seems to have been placed to command the river.

Inside, there are several brasses, and important sculptures by Rysbrack and Flaxman. But the most noteworthy feature is that the pews still carry on their backs the names of the local houses whose owners had permanent reservations: in this there's a resemblance to *Shermanbury*. The names date from the early nineteenth century, and the churchwardens have thoughtfully put up a large-scale parish map showing the whereabouts of the various houses. The reservations were for the man of the house only — womenfolk sat separately, in pews at the back of the church.

Alexander Pope and John Gay, both poets, were visitors at West Grinstead Park, but the house no longer exists, having been rebuilt in 1806. It was for years the country headquarters of the National Stud.   [10]

WESTHAM

Victims of the plague of 1666 lie in a communal grave which is rather hard to find. Step out some 15 yards from a yew in the south churchyard and you'll come across four humble and unmarked stones half buried in the ground in the form of a cross. This is the site. Inside the church (the first built by the Normans after the Conquest) is a fragment of Solomon's temple. In 1860 the vicar, Howard Hopley, visited the newly-excavated foundations of the first Temple of Jerusalem — and he shamelessly chipped off a piece of the stone!

On the village green, next to the walls of Pevensey Castle, is an old cannon on which is shown the date of its founding, 16-2-19, and the broad arrow, indicating government property, which is still in use today. It was thought unnecessary to show the century in the date, but the style of the barrel shows that it must be 1819.   [23]

WESTHAMPNETT

The famous nineteenth century cricketer, Fred Lillywhite, was born here, and he lies in the churchyard near no fewer than three bishops of Chichester. The church was Saxon in origin, and still has quite substantial traces of Saxon work; the builders used some old Roman materials. The chancel 'weeps' noticeably (see *Introduction*) and, indeed, hardly any walls meet at true right angles. Behind the vicar's stall in the chancel is a 'low side' window on whose sill are a considerable number of roughly incised pilgrims' marks. Being on a centuries-old road, it must have been regularly visited by pilgrims to the shrine of St. Richard at Chichester.   [17]

WEST HOATHLY

'Big-on-Little', or 'Great-on-Little', is in the woods near the village, and not too easy to find (best from the road near Ardingly). It's a sandstone outcrop composed of strata of unequal hardness. The softer bands underneath have eroded and now the stone has taken on a mushroom formation. Similar outcrops occur along a line which culminates in the Toadstone on Rusthall Common, a mile or so west of Tunbridge Wells and just outside our county.

A notice by the church porch directs you to the 'viewpoint', across the churchyard; and it's worth the stroll. So, too, is an amble of a few yards to the Priest House, a fifteenth century hall house built by Lewes Priory. It's now a museum of domestic bygones owned and run by the Sussex Archaeological Society. The displays include furniture, implements, toys and needlework.   [5]

WEST ITCHENOR

Itchenor is only West, it seems; no other place of the name appears on the Ordnance map. It's given over entirely to boats and yachting. The road leads right down to the water's edge, and is flanked by houses which must be devoted almost exclusively to sailing. They're attractive, though: we noticed the popularity of weeping willows. The church is unremarkable except for an astonishing western buttress which fools many people, even experts — it's quite modern. [25]

WESTMESTON

The west side of Westmeston Place, visible from the churchyard, has some fine perpendicular-style windows of about 1500. Pevsner asks where they came from: or could the house at one time have been an ecclesiastical building? The Victoria County History, which gives a good description of the house, is ignorant, too.

In the churchyard is an elaborately decorated tabernacle tomb of the Cripps family, of a type rarely met with in Sussex. Burials are recorded from 1858 to 1888, or perhaps earlier, as some of the dates are indecipherable. [20]

WEST STOKE

Twelve miles away from the other *Stokes*. Flints were mined here before the Romans came, and the nave is the original Saxo-Norman overlap (see *Introduction*) work. The tower must be almost unique, in that the point of its pyramid cap is lower than the roof ridge of the church. There's a 1635 monument inside, quite well carved. Next door is a Georgian manor house, and that's about all there is to West Stoke. [17]

WHATLINGTON

The strangely engaging Thatched Cottage has a verandah with wooden support posts, iron brackets on the walls which once perhaps held fire extinguishers, and rows of arched windows in the style known as Strawberry Hill Gothick (after the house at Twickenham which Horace Walpole had built for himself in 1750). This is an odd feature for a humble timber-framed dwelling and we're pleased to note that the building is listed.

You enter the church, unusually, through the bell tower, with steps running up to one side and the bell-ropes hanging down in front of the south door. We imagine some congestion with the ringers at work and the congregation arriving. [15]

WIGGONHOLT

The carved wooden signpost off the A283 is easily missed, and the hamlet is a cul-de-sac finishing at the church, with a neo-Georgian rectory (1959) at its side. Along the little road you pass a large house with a cupola which intrigued us. What obviously was the main drive is very overgrown, and the gates haven't been opened in years. A Roman villa has been excavated nearby; it had five rooms.   [10]

WILLINGDON

Decorating with animal bones is practised in some other parts of the country, but the only example we know of in Sussex is on the housing of the old parish pump up Wish Hill in Willingdon. Set among the flints on either side of the entrance are rows of cows' knuckle bones. They make a pleasing pattern.   [28]

WILMINGTON

'The largest representation of the human form in the world', according to some, the Long Man of Wilmington has been almost all things to all men. No-one has yet even come up with a reliable dating. Was he created in the Bronze Age, perhaps? Could he be an eighteenth century joke? These are but two of many suggestions which have been seriously advanced. And what of the two sticks in his hands? Are they possibly divining rods, or is he standing in a doorway, the lintel having eroded over the years? Back in 1873 the giant was outlined in yellow bricks to help preserve him and later, in 1969, these were replaced by the present white blocks. What we do know about him is that he is about 230 feet high and so cunningly designed that the proportions seem exactly right when you look at him, foreshortened, from the best vantage point — down below, near the car park of the eleventh century Benedictine priory.

The car park was once the tithe barn, to which the locals took a tenth of their produce for the benefit of the priest until the Tithe Commutation Act of 1836 replaced the ancient form of payment with a rent. The remains of the priory itself house a fine agricultural museum.

In the adjacent churchyard is a yew said to be a thousand years old, though yews do attract claims of this sort. What can be stated confidently is that it has a girth of 23 feet — and certainly isn't young!   [28]

WINCHELSEA

'The smallest town in England', it's said — but the claim is surely a form of whistling in the dark. It *was* a true town in the twelfth century when (along with Hastings and Rye) it was one of the powerful cinque ports which provided men and ships for successive monarchs in return for hard cash and special privileges. A series of misfortunes befell Winchelsea, however, and today, although it still boasts a mayor and corporation, it is but a shadow (albeit a most attractive shadow) of its former self.

The first catastrophe was a natural one. During the thirteenth century Winchelsea was virtually destroyed by terrible storms. Edward the First ordered a new town some miles away, on the present site. A planner's dream, this was to be built on a grid of 39 squares, only a dozen of which were ever completed. The second disaster was not long in coming — raids by the French which devastated Winchelsea in 1360, 1380 and, yet again, in 1449. The third, and decisive, blow was the retreat of the sea and the silting up of the harbour. By the middle of the sixteenth century Winchelsea, marooned, was no longer a port.

Three of the medieval gates remain, and the position of New Gate, across the fields far to the south, gives an indication of the town's former size and glory. The Look Out, near the Strand Gate, offers a view of the whole of Romney Marsh. Many of the Georgian buildings stand on medieval undercrofts and cellars, while some of the best Franciscan remains in the country can be seen in the grounds of the private house, Greyfriars. There is an excellent visitors' guide on a board close to the (substantial) remains of the church.   [24]

WINDMILL HILL

No prizes for guessing the outstanding feature of this place, which before the sixteenth century was known as Posey Green. Far from the most beautiful example in the county, the derelict metal-clad postmill is nonetheless impressive for its sheer size: it measures about 50 feet from the ground to the roof ridge.   [23]

150

WINEHAM

George Bernard Shaw did some of his writing at the house called Mercers, which is worth more than a glance on its own account. Built for a wealthy family in 1485, it's tile-hung with a Horsham slab roof and huge chimneys. There's a small lake in the garden. Wineham has no church, but a fenced gap in the hedge at the house called Gatefield was once the entrance to a mission hall. You can make out on the ground where it would have stood.   [11]

WISBOROUGH GREEN

The Arun Navigation section here is dry and overgrown, and you can walk it. Orfold Aqueduct (reached by path from Orfold Farm) carries the Navigation over the river Arun. It's built of brick with three arches, and acts as a weir on the river. Immediately to the north of this, the walls of Orfold Lock (or Lording's Lock) on the Arun are well preserved.

The church, perched up on the only rising ground in sight, is a good object for architectural detective work. The off-centre tower, cutting across the interior of one of the windows, takes a lot of explaining.

On the west side of the green, almost opposite a garage, is the Zoar Chapel, dated 1753 in quaint figures over the door. A couple of plots away is the old graveyard, with a full anthology of carvings — cherubs, serpents, hour-glasses, trumpets, skulls-and-crossbones, all are there.   [9]

WITHYHAM

'Duckings' is the show house here, a little east of the Dorset Arms. It dates from the mid-Tudor period, and judging by the adjacent hammer-pond it must have been lived in by, and perhaps built for, an ironmaster. It isn't just picturesque: it's an important piece of the architecture of its time.

But the main interest in Withyham must centre upon the church, set high above the main road. It contains the broad and splendid Sackville Chapel, with many memorials to the Sackville and de la Warr families. Beneath the Renaissance painted ceiling hang six great banners, and below them, in the middle of the floor, Cibber's great sculptured monument to Thomas Sackville, a boy of thirteen at his death in 1677. Life-sized marble figures kneel at each side on cushions set on the tomb steps, so that you can kneel beside them. Round the walls are works by several top names among English sculptors — Chantrey, Flaxman, Nollekens. Here, too, repose the ashes of Vita Sackville-West, the authoress and poet, who was born at Knole and died at Sissinghurst, on June 2, 1962. She was the wife of historian Harold Nicolson.

By the font is a very rustic iron grave slab, which reads, brokenly:

Here lieth Willyam Alfrey
late of Wythiham
Yeoman which ende
d his life the 15 day
of June Anno Do. 1610

WITTERINGS, The

There are two, East and West, with Cakeham in between. Along the shore are several massive erratic boulders — chunks of worn granites, gneiss, basalt and other non-local rocks (see *Rustington*). The nearest spot from which they could have come is in the Channel Isles, and they must have been carried here by a glacier during one of the great Ice Ages.

The church has an interesting rarity — the tomb of a boy bishop. In the middle ages a chorister was chosen as a kind of mock-bishop for the three weeks or so before Christmas; he was fully robed and treated exactly as if he were the real bishop. This poor mite must have died in office. Only one other tomb of a boy-bishop is to be found in England, at Salisbury.

Just off East Wittering high street stand the remains of a brick tower mill, now overgrown, which started its work about 1810 and went on until its sweeps (the 'sails') were removed at the end of the century. The interior fitments were destroyed by fire in 1975, but the sturdy brick cone still dominates the shopping centre. The road almost opposite leads to the new parish church; the old one is a good half mile outside the village and is locked, being no longer used for services. It has a fine Norman south door.

[25]

WIVELSFIELD

Murder most foul — and its dire consequences. The Royal Oak Inn sign carries a subtitle, as it were: 'Jacob's Post'. Sure enough, in the back garden is the post itself, held up by three stays. And who was Jacob? His full name was Jacob Harris, and he was a pedlar from Horsham. In 1734 he rode to the inn and proceeded to murder the host and his wife and a maidservant. Harris was captured and executed at Horsham — he was hung in chains close to the scene of the murders, and it's a part of that gibbet which you can see. It's far smaller than it was, because for years splinters were picked off it by country folk who held to the belief that a piece of wood from a gibbet was an infallible remedy for toothache!

The B2112 from Ditchling crosses Ditchling Common, at the north end of which is the Wivelsfield village sign. Almost at once you meet the remains of an old gate-post which must in days past have held up a barrier across the road. It may have been a farm-gate or a toll-gate; old Ordnance maps fail to show it, though the road is marked on maps at least back to 1724.

A puzzle — in the belfry chamber of Wivelsfield church, on the wall, is a gravestone with an inscription of which two lines are upside down. Can you suggest why? *We make our guess as to the reason on page 161* [11]

WOOLAVINGTON

Also called East Lavington, Woolavington is the old hundred name rather than a place. The church lies at the end of a long cul-de-sac, and has now been taken over as the chapel for adjoining Seaford College. It has been modernised to conform with school requirements, but hasn't lost its character. Look at the bosses on each side of the chancel roof; they're modern, and are decorated with the Keys of the Kingdom at the east end, and the Symbols of the Passion on the other four. The choir stalls have four misericords (see *Etchingham*). In a case in the south transept is a magnificent crozier. [9]

WOOLBEDING

Older guide-books say that there's a fine avenue of yew trees to the church. Alas, no longer: there are just five against the south wall of the churchyard. A replacement avenue of saplings has been planted, but none of us is likely to see them in their maturity. This is more encouraging than the conservation work to the tower. Presumably in an effort to give a rather flat tower a bit of surface texture, when it was last re-pointed the workmen stuck dark brown pebbles every two or three inches along the fresh cement. It looks almost as if the rector's wife had burnt the toast and put that in. All the same the church, which has a lot of Saxon work, is well worth exploring — if you can find the key.

In the churchyard is the grave of the Rev. Francis Bourdillon, who died in April 1912 at the age of 94. He was the author of 'Alone with God' and other popular books of their day. [8]

WORTH

One of the really important churches in the whole country — the largest and best-preserved Saxon church that can be found. A church was here as early as King Alfred's time, but the present one is of the tenth or eleventh century, with all the generosity of style of that period. The chancel arch is almost overpoweringly massive, and the details of Saxon workmanship in carving and decoration make it a 'must' for lovers of this earliest of Christian art. The tower, however, is Victorian and out-of-place.

Notice how the church has separate courses of footings to the exterior of its walls, making much of the building look as if it were standing on a plinth. Notice, too, the sixteenth century lych-gate, which was restored in 1956. Much of its timber is still in place, and the stone roof is splendid.[4]

WYCH CROSS

A place for milestone curiosities. The turnpike trusts formed in the eighteenth century to improve the road networks were punctilious about erecting milestones along their routes, but at Wych Cross there's been the oddity of *two* cast iron posts each claiming to be 35 miles from the City of London (note the punning allusion to Bow Bells on most of the stones — a bow of ribbon with bells beneath). The reason is that road improvements in Surrey early in the nineteenth century added about half a mile to the journey, but the Wych Cross trustees refused to shift their markers to compensate. Their neighbours to the north *did* move theirs and therefore had to introduce a new stone for 35 miles — you'll see that it has a honeysuckle design rather than the bells. The older 35-mile post vanished during the period in which we were writing this book: we can only hope that it will reappear.

This sequence of original milestones along the A22 from East Grinstead to Hailsham is the longest in the county, but there are others on the A26 between Uckfield and Lewes; on the A268 between Northiam and Rye; and on the B2026 north of Duddleswell.

Also at Wych Cross, on the triangle of green between the A22 and the A275, is a sandstone slab which was once in the wall of a tollhouse here. It's inscribed: 'To Marsfield 6 Miles/from Marsfield to Uckfield 1 Mile half/from Uckfield to Lewes 7 Miles half/ and this is the Toll Road to Lewes.' Marsfield is, of course, Maresfield. [12]

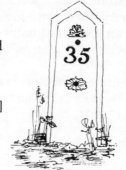 

YAPTON

The word 'quaint' really fits the old church, as it's full of funny angles. The tower west buttress has another buttress growing sideways out of it, and the lower west window of the tower slants to an alarming degree. Between the north wall of the tower and the nave is an unexpected length of roof which also slants away. And the porch leans right forward as if about to nod off. But it must be a later addition — see how the porch roof-ridge projects above the line of the sill of the west window.

Our last entry ought at least to give a hint of refreshment awaiting us, and what better than the Yapton local, The Shoulder of Mutton and Cucumbers? Not surprisingly, it's the only pub with this bizarre name in the entire country. We raise a glass to our hidden, and curious, Sussex![18]

Books for the record . . .

Here are some of the books we have used, which you may like to know of if you want to go exploring the places you have been reading about.

Certain books have been with us on all our travels: Nairn and Pevsner, 'The Buildings of England — Sussex' (Pelican); K. Spence, 'The Companion Guide to Kent and Sussex' (Collins); M. H. C. Baker, 'Sussex Villages' (Hale). Some have been too bulky, but invaluable at home: The Victoria County History of Sussex (seven volumes so far published); P. Brandon (ed.), 'The South Saxons' (Phillimore); Mawer and Stenton, 'The Place-names of Sussex' (Cambridge).

Books more for reading and less as guides have filled in a great number of gaps in our background, and we have blessed them often. They've included J. Burke, 'Sussex' and B. Willard, 'Sussex' (both Batsford); D. Harrison, 'Along the South Downs' (Cassell); J. R. Armstrong, 'A History of Sussex' (Phillimore); P. Brandon, 'The Sussex Landscape' (Hodder & Stoughton); and M. Goldsworthy, 'The Sussex Bedside Anthology' (Arundel Press).

A few books have been invaluable in providing clues for visits and research, but have been too marred by factual inaccuracies to be reliable. Among these are: A. Mee, 'The King's England — Sussex', and N. Wymer, 'Companion into Sussex'. The most comprehensive coverage of places and how to get there was provided by F. R. Banks, 'Sussex' (The Penguin Guides, 1957 — now out of print), though even that doesn't mention all the places we've visited.

Books on specialised aspects of our explorations include: J. Dyer, 'Southern England, An Archaeological Guide' (Faber); M. Brunnarius, 'The Windmills of Sussex' (Phillimore); A. J. Haselfoot, 'Guide to the Industrial Archaeology of South-East England' (Batsford); A. Barr-Hamilton, 'In Saxon Sussex' (Arundel Press); M. G. Welch, 'Early Anglo-Saxon Sussex' (BAR, Oxford); E. Straker, 'Wealden Iron' (first published 1931, reprinted David & Charles); R. & R. McDermott, 'The Standing Windmills of Sussex' — separate volumes for East and West Sussex (McDermott); and 'Sussex River' (3 volumes) and 'Another Sussex River', both by indefatigable columnists Edna and 'Mac' McCarthy (Lindel). A book on its own for scholarship, accuracy and amusement is W. D. Parish, 'A Dictionary of the Sussex Dialect' (Gardner's of Bexhill).

Older books which we've been able to collect include Histories of Sussex by Dallaway & Cartwright (West only), T. W. Horsfield and M. A. Lower; Rev. P. de Putron, 'Nooks and Corners of Old Sussex'; Rev. A. Hussey, 'Churches of Kent, Sussex and Surrey'; A. H. Peat and L. C. Halsted, 'Churches and other Antiquities of West Sussex'; Sussex Guides by Augustus J. C. Hare (1896), Sawyer (Black, 1892) and Ward and Baxter (Nelson, 1913); and a whole series by Rev. A. A. Evans.

And that's only a few. The list would be incomplete without mention of the 1:50,000 series of Ordnance maps (seven cover the whole county, sheets nos. 186, 187, 188, 189, 197, 198, 199), and quite literally hundreds of village and church guides, old and new. They've all come in handy, and we're most grateful.

INDEX OF SUBJECTS

(Not including references in the Introduction)

158

Cross Bush
Jevington
Milland
Possingworth
Pulborough
Runcton
Rusper
Rushlake Green
South Malling

Monsters
Colgate
Lyminster
Maresfield
Selham

Monuments in Churches & Churchyards
Ashington
Brightling
Broadwater
Chiddingly
Clapham
Cocking
Henfield
Horsted Keynes
Hurst Green
Jevington
Playden
Slaugham
Slindon
Terwick
Thakeham
West Grinstead
West Stoke
Withyham

Monuments, Secular
Heathfield
Iden
Patcham
Peacehaven
Piltdown
Pulborough

Mosaic
Bignor
East Hoathly
Fishbourne
Tarring, West

Museums
Bignor
Bramber
Cuckfield
Exceat
Fishbourne
Halland
Heathfield
Houghton
Mayfield
Midhurst
Northiam
Playden
Polegate
Preston
Rottingdean
Sedlescombe
Singleton
Southover
Tangmere
Tarring, West
Warnham
West Chiltington
West Hoathly
Wilmington

Musical Instruments
(*and see* ORGANS)
Ashurst
Brede

Buxted
Kingston Buci
Mundham

Musicians & Composers
Amberley
Fittleworth
Folkington
Friston
Icklesham
Rusper
Storrington

Names & Name-Signs
Bargham
Barlavington
Coldwaltham
Faygate
Halland
Kingston Buci
Kirdford
Mardens, The
Mayfield
Minsted
Ninfield
Pevensey
Rye Foreign
Tarring Neville
Warninglid

National Trust
Alfriston
Bodiam
Burwash
Ditchling
Handcross
Harting
Newtimber
Rodmell
Selsfield
Sheffield Park

Natural Features
(*and see* BEACONS)
Amberley
Birling
Blackdown
Bracklesham
Exceat
Houghton
Iford
Rustington
Telscombe
West Hoathly
Wittering, West

Nature Reserves
Coldwaltham
Pagham
Small Dole
Ticehurst

Newspapers & Press
Ifield
Rottingdean
Upper Dicker

Oasts
Boreham Street
Groombridge

Orangery
Eartham

Organs, Church
Appledram
Brightling
Ringmer

Ottawa
Frant

Painters
Berwick
Brightling

Charleston
Ditchling
Handcross
Houghton
Parham
Rottingdean
West Blatchington

Paintings in Churches
Aldingbourne
Arlington
Berwick
Brede
Brightling
Clayton
Climping
Cocking
Coleman's Hatch
Coombes
Hardham
Netherfield
Ovingdean
Plumpton
Rotherfield
Staplefield
Trotton
West Chiltington

Pews
Dallington
Didling
Eridge
Folkington
Heyshott
Parham
Shermanbury
Warbleton
Warminghurst
West Grinstead

Pillery
Storrington

Poets
(*see* AUTHORS)

Politicians, Statesmen
Bramber
Eartham
Easthampnett
Folkington
Heyshott
Rottingdean
Walberton

Ponds & Lakes
(*and see* HAMMERPONDS)
Battle
Boarshead
Chanctonbury
Ditchling
Falmer
Hammerpot
Lower Beeding
Lyminster
Milland
Newtimber
Plaistow
Upper Dicker
Warnham

Porches
Billingshurst
Bishopstone
Icklesham
Linchmere
Lindfield
Lurgashall
Poynings
Westfield
Yapton

Ports
(*see* HARBOURS)

Postal
Bodle Street
Hickstead

Pottery
Arlington
Buxted
Fishbourne
Lower Dicker
Pagham
Singleton

Pounds
Kingston (East Sussex)
Sidlesham

Prehistoric Remains
(*and see* FLINTS)
Beddingham
Bepton
Chanctonbury
Compton
Ditchling
Findon
Goodwood
Hurstpierpoint
Mark Cross
Nepcote
Piltdown (hoax)
Plumpton
Stoughton
Wannock

Priest Houses
Alfriston
Coldwaltham
Denton
Itchingfield
Merston
West Hoathly

Priests & Preachers
Coneyhurst
Iden
Rudgwick
Selmeston
Upwaltham
Warbleton
Warminghurst
Westham

Priories
(*and see* ABBEYS, MONASTERIES)
Boxgrove
Easebourne
Hardham
Lyminster
Sayers Common
Shulbrede
Southover
Tortington
Upper Beeding
Wilmington
Winchelsea

Proverbs & Sayings
Cocking
Selsey

Pulpits
Broadwater
Frant
Newick
Patching
Rotherfield
Warminghurst

Pumps, Water
Burpham
Falmer
Littleworth
Newick

Cakeham
Crossbush
Donnington
Handcross
Heathfield
Hurst Green
Iford
Laughton
Litlington
Mark Cross
Partridge Green
Piddinghoe
Pulborough
Rogate
Selsfield
Sompting
Southease
Tillington
Upperton
Washington
West Stoke
Whatlington
Wisborough Green
Woolbeding
Town Development
Peacehaven
Winchelsea
Town Halls
Pevensey
Steyning
Trees
Barnham
Botolphs
Chailey
Chanctonbury
Coates
Crowhurst
Forest Row
Hurstpierpoint
Kingston (West Sussex)
Little Horsted
Lodsworth
Newtimber

Northiam
Stansted
Stedham
Streat
Sullington
Uckfield
Udimore
Westbourne
West Dean (West Sussex)
West Itchenor
Wilmington
Woolbeding
Tunnels
Clayton
Halland
Hardham
Milland
Offham
Pyecombe
South Heighton
Tide Mills
Viewpoints
Bargham
Beddingham
Bepton
Dell Quay
Didling
Ditchling
Hooe
Linchmere
Nepcote
Piddinghoe
Southease
Sullington
Telscombe
West Hoathly
Vineyards
Horam
Waldron
Walls
Buxted
Catsfield
Ford

Glynde
Henfield
Offham
West Dean (East Sussex)
War Relics
Ford
Southease
South Heighton
Tangmere
Westham
Water & Watercourses
(*and see* CANALS, PONDS, RIVERS)
Albourne
Ardingly
Balcombe
Felpham
Fulking
Ticehurst
Watermills
Albourne
Birdham
Bracklesham
Burton
Burwash
Duncton
Iping
Lurgashall
Sidlesham
Tide Mills
Walstead
Weathervanes
Hadlow Down
Merston
Piddinghoe
Wells
East Marden
Littleworth
Windmills
(*P=Post, S=Smock, T=Tower*)

Barnham	T
Chailey	P
Clayton	P, T

Climping	S
Cross-in-Hand	P
Dell Quay	P
Earnley	S
Goodwood	?
Halnaker	T
High Salvington	P
Icklesham	P
Keymer	P
Mayfield	P
Nutbourne	T
Nutley	P
Nyetimber	T
Polegate	T
Punnett's Town	S
Rottingdean	S
Shipley	S
Stone Cross	T
West Blatchington	S
West Chiltington	S
Windmill Hill	P
Wittering, East	T

Windows
Chalvington
Climping
Cuckfield
Ewhurst Green
Framfield
Lancing
Lodsworth
Pagham
Rodmell
Stoke, North
Twineham
Westmeston
Whatlington
Woods & Forests
Arlington
Coleman's Hatch
Colgate
Exceat
Lower Dicker

That Wivelsfield conundrum . . . We don't know whether we're right, but our guess is that the mason started to carve the bit which is now upside down — the lettering is older in style. Then he made a spelling mistake in the Latin, as you can read if you know any Latin, so he chucked it aside and started a fresh piece of stone. Years later, using a more modern lettering, he or another mason started again the other way up, and finished it. The mishap at the other end of the stone wouldn't show since it would be underground. Now, we wonder what *really* happened!

POSTSCRIPT

Our pleasure at the need for a third printing within eight months is compounded by the quite unexpected attention already given to a number of the objects we feature. The white horse of our Litlington entry has been lovingly groomed by the Conservation Volunteers (compare it with the 'before' sketch below); the little church ruin at Binderton is being repaired; while East Sussex County Council is planning to give the Brightling Needle a much-needed face-lift. May these renovations be the first of many!

Several readers have written to us with comments, suggestions and (mercifully few) slaps on the wrist, and we include some of their observations in our notes below. Since the books are obviously being well used, we have improved the finish of this edition so that they are even better able to withstand the rigours of constant thumbings on innumerable country jaunts.

Introduction. Page 9, line 9. For 'Baptist' read 'Evangelist'.
Page 12. Dicul belongs to Bosham, not Boxgrove, as the village entry makes clear.

Angmering. Motorists' fatigue! We mean, of course, the A259.

Anstye. Note the curious village sign which testifies to an apparent controversy. The name is spelt both with and without the final 'e'. *(Near Cuckfield)*

Blackstone. Praise is due to the village for preserving the old well in its former humble condition — unadvertised on the roadside verge. *(Near Henfield)*

Broadwater. For 'churchyard' read 'cemetery'.

Bury. We overestimated the period of the ferry's desuetude, 'over a quarter of a century' being nearer the mark. (Even a local resident can give you wrong information!)

Chailey. Add to the Greenwich Meridian marker at Peacehaven the one on Lane End Common. Turn right off the A275 just short of Sheffield Park station and it's about 30 yards along on your left. The wording repeats that 'centre of Sussex' boast.

Crowborough. No more letters, please, about the height of the beacon, for which we've seen a variety of figures. 'About 800 feet' should satisfy everyone.

Etchingham. The copper weather-vane on the church is contemporary with the building itself (14th century) and may be the oldest in England.

Hartfield. Map reference should be **5/6**.

Rustington. The clock was at Great Bedwyn from 1769 to 1905 — rather less than 200 years.

Scaynes Hill. Freshfield Halt was set up by the Bluebell Railway but is no longer in existence. Cars using it became a danger.

Tortington. Delete 'fan'. (Perhaps it's lierne vaulting?)

Udimore. Our entry under Boreham Street indicates that we meant to mention oast houses at Udimore (space prevented us). One of the farms near the village has a central square of buildings with an oast house at each corner. The resultant effect is rather like a romantic medieval castle.

Washington. Off with our heads! It was in Henry the Seventh's reign.

Withyham. Map reference **5/6**.